SEVENTEENTH-CENTURY LITERATURE AND CULTURE

INTRODUCTIONS TO BRITISH LITERATURE
AND CULTURE SERIES

Introductions to British Literature and Culture are
practical guides to key literary periods. Guides in the series
are designed to help introduce a new module or area of
study, providing concise information on the historical,
literary and critical contexts and acting as an initial map of
the knowledge needed to study the literature and culture of
a specific period. Each guide includes an overview of the
historical period, intellectual contexts, major genres, critical
approaches and a guide to original research and resource
materials in the area, enabling students to progress
confidently to further study.

FORTHCOMING TITLES

Medieval Literature and Culture by Andrew Galloway

Renaissance Literature and Culture by Lisa Hopkins and
   Matthew Steggle

Eighteenth-Century Literature and Culture by Paul Goring

Romanticism by Sharon Ruston

Victorian Literature and Culture by Maureen Moran

Modernism by Leigh Wilson

Postwar British Literature and Culture 1945–1980 by Susan
   Brook

Contemporary British Literature and Culture by Sean Matthews

SEVENTEENTH-CENTURY LITERATURE AND CULTURE

Jim Daems

continuum

Continuum
The Tower Building
11 York Road
London SE1 7NX

80 Maiden Lane
Suite 704
New York, NY 10038

www.continuumbooks.com

© Jim Daems 2006

British Library Cataloguing-in-Publication Data
A catalogue record for this book is available from the British Library.

ISBN 10: 0-8264-8658-4 (hardback)
          0-8264-8659-2 (paperback)

ISBN 13: 978-08264-8658-5 (hardback)
          978-08264-8659-2 (paperback)

Library of Congress Cataloging-in-Publication Data
A catalog record for this book is available from the Library of Congress.

Typeset by Servis Filmsetting Ltd, Manchester
Printed and bound in Great Britain by MPG Books Ltd, Bodmin, Cornwall

Contents

Introduction

A century is a convenient, but arbitrary, division of time. It implies a distinct beginning, middle and end. Perhaps more so than the preceding centuries, seventeenth-century literature and culture comprise a number of beginnings and endings. There is continuity, for example, in the early decades of the century with the last decade of the sixteenth century in the work of writers such as John Donne and, particularly, William Shakespeare and Ben Jonson. This has prompted many scholars to locate the end of the English Renaissance period at 1640 when Parliament ordered the public theatres closed. In addition, the Neoclassicism of John Dryden during the Restoration has resulted in the appropriation of the closing decades of the seventeenth century into the 'long eighteenth century' (1660 to the emergence of Romanticism). But these divisions (which trim the century covered in this book to 85 years) are symptomatic of the period itself and the divisive struggles that are its history. I would like, then, in the next couple of pages, broadly to sketch out the continuities and disruptions that this book will discuss.

As a period, 1603 to 1688 is marked by significant political and religious turmoil in England, Scotland, Wales and Ireland. Conflict between king and Parliament in the first half of the century – at the best of times a strained relationship during James I's reign – came to a head when Charles I called Parliament in 1640. Two years later, the civil wars began. Charles I would be executed in 1649, and monarchy abolished. But 11 years of political experimentation was unable to arrive at a suitable settlement. In addition, the 1640s and 1650s witnessed the rapid rise of political and religious radicalism, which even alarmed many supporters of the revolution. Taking advantage of a lapse in effective press censorship, radical groups seized the opportunity to present their case to the reading public. However, with the collapse of the Protectorate shortly after Oliver Cromwell's death, it appeared that only a monarch could ensure social stability. Charles II was restored in 1660 amidst widespread popular rejoicing and, in the following years, the majority of the more radical groups would pass quickly, and often quietly, into history.

Religion had played an important part in these events. Many felt that through the first half of the century, Puritanism had contributed greatly to the Civil War. So, too, did anti-Catholicism. And though the restoration of Charles II was celebrated, and the Church of England's authority reinstated with the aid of Parliament, religious tensions continued to threaten to tear the Stuart kingdoms apart, particularly during the Popish Plot and the Exclusion Crisis. Fears of 'popery' came to a head with the accession of the Catholic James II in 1685. His reign, however, would be cut short by the Glorious Revolution. Throughout the century, accompanying these political and religious tensions, developments in science and philosophy would also call into question long-held beliefs regarding authority. The upheaval of the civil wars and execution of Charles I, along with new ideas in politics, religion, philosophy and science, forced people to perceive their world differently.

Seventeenth-century literature engages with this. In poetry, drama and prose the dissolution of once-unquestioned beliefs can be strongly felt. In drama, the period witnessed Shakespeare's great tragedies and innovative romances, which most certainly intervene in Jacobean political and religious debates. Some critics today even suggest that Jacobean and Caroline tragic playwrights enact the gradual de-sacralization of kingship in the radical questions posed within this genre.

Comic playwrights came to focus on the corruption of London. City comedies reveal the concerns many had about an increasingly mercenary, materialistic world which challenged notions of class and gender identity. At court, the masque achieved its most fabulous heights during the reigns of James I and Charles I, providing spectacularly choreographed celebrations of an idealized, benevolent reign. Playwrights were also finding a new, more exclusive audience in the private theatres, one which favoured tragi-comedy. And, when the public theatres reopened at the Restoration, after an 18-year closure by order of Parliament, the tastes of theatre goers came to favour the comedy of manners, heroic drama and, to us, barely recognizable adaptations of Shakespeare made to fit the changing taste in dramatic theory.

Poetry and prose also bear the mark of social turmoil. In poetry, the Metaphysical poets – John Donne and those he influenced – challenged earlier poetic conventions which had become clichéd. Much of this was a response not only to the stagnation of poetic modes, but also a concerted effort to devise a new means of poetic expression in the face of change. Even Ben Jonson, in his aggressive appropriation of the classics, realized that the social standing of the poet could only be raised by engaging with his society. The poets he most strongly influenced, the Cavaliers, extended Jonson's poetic and made the poet's pen analogous to the sword – asserting and defending a monarchy in crisis. Through the last half of the century, John Milton and Andrew Marvell worked toward a republican poetic. While, after the Restoration, a restrained Augustan poetic would come to be formulated by John Dryden to reassert the centrality of the monarch to social order and to satirize brilliantly the excesses of the Whigs. In prose, the breakdown of authority in mid-century, and the consequent collapse of press censorship, allowed for the creation of a radicalized public sphere. The newsbook – the forerunner of our newspapers – responded to a developing, insatiable desire for news. Controversial political and religious polemic also flowed from the presses, including writings challenging the subordinate status of women. Even in fictional prose genres, particularly romance, authors engaged with contemporary debates throughout the century.

An introductory book of this length requires concision. The structure of this book is, in large part, chronological. Chapter 1 explores the cultural, political, religious and intellectual contexts of the period. Chapter 2 consists of individual sections dealing with poetry, drama and prose, and concludes with a discussion of literary movements. Chapter 3 provides a historical overview of literary criticism as well as current critical debates. Hence, the book is structured in an accessible way which allows students to trace developments readily over the 85 years it covers. Selecting what to include, as in any book, will always reflect the biases of the author. What is here most certainly reflects my own approach to teaching the literature of this period. However, the chronology and suggested readings in the Resources at the end of the book provide helpful pointers to students, both in order to further their understanding of issues raised, as well as to assist them in pursuing their own research interests. Some of the resources it includes are, conveniently, web-based.

Finally, I would like to acknowledge the assistance of Dr Holly Faith Nelson, who kindly read the manuscript at an early stage and provided many helpful suggestions; as did an anonymous reader at Continuum.

1

Historical, Cultural and Intellectual Contexts

ARTS AND CULTURE

Popular culture

Popular and court culture dynamically coexisted through the socio-political turmoil of the period. Though popular and court cultural forms, both reinforced by the liturgical calendar of the Church of England, could, ideally, work together to strengthen the hierarchical bonds of society, they could also come into conflict. Often, this resulted from a clash

between Puritans and the political and ecclesiastical authorities who firmly upheld a paternalistic notion of reciprocal
community: the benevolent obligations of the ruling class
and the wilful submission of the monarch's subjects. Puritans
opposed the rites, ceremonies and forms of worship of the
Church of England, many of which they saw as remnants of
England's Catholic past. They felt that the reformation
begun in Henry VIII's reign had not been completed. In
addition, Puritans felt that many popular folk beliefs, such as
May Day celebrations, were 'pagan' and, therefore, ungodly.
Puritan opposition manifested itself not only in the strictly
political sphere of petitioning for reforms and, increasingly,
parliamentary debate, but also on a localized level – the
parish, town or city. The Church of England and the
monarch, however, attempted to manage popular festivals
and traditional entertainments at a local level in order to
inspire loyalty.

For the Church and the monarchy, the benefits of allowing the lower orders to celebrate holy-days and political occasions, as well as rural events centring upon the natural cycle
of planting and harvesting, accrued to the hierarchical social
order. While the links between popular culture and the intentions of the ruling class 'must always reflect the ambiguity
inherent in activities whose objectives are rarely expressed
explicitly and whose impact is beyond quantification' (Kelsey
1997, p. 78), regal authority was naturalized – made to seem
a manifest part of the divine order of the cosmos – through
the liturgical and seasonal cycles. The importance of traditional culture and pastimes to the ruling class is evident in
James I's Declaration of Sports (1618), reissued by Charles I
in 1633. The Declaration denounced 'Puritans and precise
people' for 'prohibiting and unlawful punishing of our good
people for using their lawful recreations and honest exercises'
(Gardiner 1951, p. 100). Puritans viewed such pastimes as
both pagan and 'popish', but their attempts to curtail them
met with limited success for two reasons. First, such festivities
and celebrations were, in many localities, deeply ingrained.
Second, any attempt by Puritans to prohibit traditional

culture was dependant upon the support of the local elite to whom they appealed on the basis of 'godly' reformation. It was simply not in the best interests of many of these men to give heed to the Puritan critique, as their authority went hand in hand with the Church and the king. But even a Puritan ascendancy in local or civic government did not necessarily bring about the total extirpation of traditional culture; rather, it would often be reformed in order to assert a more 'godly' sense of authority.

Traditional popular culture also continued to thrive in the middle of the century. During the civil wars and Interregnum, 'traditional culture was commonly perceived as being (and often was, in fact) associated with counter-revolutionary notions about the proper ordering of Church and State – with the beliefs and rituals of episcopacy and monarchy' (Underdown 1987, p. 239). As David Underdown has demonstrated, the association of popular pastimes with the Stuarts was assumed by both Cavalier and Parliamentarian alike. This link would continue, and become more openly practised, throughout the seventeenth century; for example, upon Charles II's restoration, May Day celebrations effectively reasserted the monarchical social order with popular festivity. Samuel Pepys (1960, p. 23) noted in his diary that 1 May 1660 'will be remembered for the happiest May-day that hath been many a year to England'. Many popular celebrations marking the Restoration also included the roasting of 'rumps' of meat in derision of the Rump Parliament created by Pride's Purge. In fact, as political events were tending towards the Restoration, the Duke of Newcastle (Rudrum *et al.* 2001b, p. 235) reminded Charles II that such 'divertissements will amuse the people's thoughts, and keep them in harmless action which will free your Majesty from faction and rebellion'.

Court culture: King and protector

In contrast to popular culture, the court employed much more opulent cultural forms in order to represent its authority.

The centre of this culture was the king's primary residence, Whitehall Palace – the term palace, however, needs to be clarified as regards Whitehall. It had been acquired by Henry VIII from Cardinal Wolsey in 1529 and, by 1603, it had become a sprawl of buildings in Westminster, rather than having been built to a coherently designed architectural plan. In the mid-century, 'one survey counted well over a thousand rooms, fifty-five closets, seventy-five garrets, twenty-six cellars and thirsteen kitchens' (Kelsey 1997, p. 41). The Stuarts never had the money to rebuild it, though Inigo Jones had drawn up preliminary plans. Its sprawl was in large part due to the army of people necessary to maintain Whitehall's four principal functions. First, it was a royal residence serving the needs of the king and his family. Second, it represented the magnificence of the realm to the world – foreign ambassadors and visiting dignitaries – as well as to the king's subjects. This was accomplished through a yearly cycle of ceremonies and ritual. Third, Whitehall was the centre of both cultural and political patronage. Finally, it was the political centre of the realm not only because of the presence of the king, but also of his chief officers, who operated from its precincts.

It is important to keep in mind, however, that while the king was the main influence on the court, in many ways he was also defined by it. The central figure of court life, be he king or protector:

> stamped his personality and preferences on the court: through those he promoted, and in the ordinances he chose to enforce or allowed to lapse. Conversely, however, the court also imposed its own disciplines on the prince. Court life revolved around ritual.
> (Adamson 2000, pp. 99–100)

The liturgical calendar of the Church of England regulated life at court as much as it did life in the city and countryside. There were also rituals specific to the court. These include basic forms of etiquette amongst courtiers, how one was to behave in the presence of the king or a member of the royal family and at ceremonies. Two of the most elaborate ceremonials were the Order of the Garter installations and processions, which Charles I re-established in its full dignity, and 'touching for the king's evil', a form of tuberculosis with a naturally high recovery rate. The elaborate ritual involved the king, surrounded by clergy and court officials, in his mystical, divine role as the earthly mediator of God; all the Stuart monarchs until 1688 performed this rite.

To further understand the court's character, we might briefly consider the moral climate of the Stuart courts through a contrast of James I and Charles I. James I was noted for his public fawning over his male favourites, such as George Villiers, who quickly rose to Duke of Buckingham. Even if we turn to a hostile observer, Charles I's court was an orderly one. Lucy Hutchinson (1995, p. 67), in the memoir of her husband, a signatory of Charles I's death warrant, described the moral climate in the Caroline court in this way:

> Charles was temperate and chaste and serious, so that the fools and bawds, mimics and catamites of the former court grew out of fashion, and the nobility and courtiers, who did not quite abandon their debaucheries, had yet the reverence to the King to retire into corners to practice them.

Charles I 'set a personal example of comeliness and sobriety at court, so in turn, the court, reflecting his virtues, would become the model for the country' (Sharpe 1989, p. 171). Indeed,

> Charles excluded the openly scandalous from his court, and his personal morality reflected the respectful and monogamous regard for his wife, Henrietta Maria, which found expression in the encouragement of a cult of idealized Platonic love and in the celebration of their reign as an equal partnership.
>
> (Corns 1992, p. 203)

In this way, the royal union was to symbolize the ideal, loving relationship of the king to his realm.

Following the execution of Charles I, ritual, pageantry and theatricality were not tossed into the dustbin of history. As Sean Kelsey (1997, p. 26) has demonstrated, the Commonwealth 'showed a consistently enthusiastic and increasingly confident commitment to restoring the charismatic focus of civilian government, bringing back some of the gloss of traditional patterns of authority tarnished by revolution'. In contrast to Charles I, whose fastidious sense of privacy meant that he rarely went on public display, the Commonwealth and Protectorate regimes were more visible, appropriating aristocratic forms of representation in order to add a familiarity to their own authority. During the Commonwealth, Whitehall Palace continued to be the centre of government, while with the Protectorate, it once again served as the principal residence of a quasi-monarchical figure. Incidentally, as the Protector, Oliver Cromwell took up residence in Whitehall; he also received Hampton Court Palace.

In the Protectoral palaces, court etiquette was reinstituted and, in 1655, the office of Lord Chamberlain was recreated and four gentlemen of the bedchamber were appointed for the Lord Protector. Cultural forms also portrayed the regime in ways very similar to a monarchical court. In portraiture, for example, parliamentarians were painted by many of the same artists who had painted, and continued to paint, aristocrats. The style, too, stayed much the same. In this way, the premier painters of the middle of the century – Robert Walker, Samuel Cooper and Peter Lely – provided a familiar aura of authority in portraits of Cromwell. Cromwell also patronized musicians. Masques were even performed at court, primarily at diplomatic functions, as Whitehall once again began to serve its principal functions. Hence, although the kingly office had been abolished, the Protectorate essentially restored older forms of allegiance and deference. The quasi-regal dignity created at Whitehall around Cromwell meant that the court operated in much the same way as under a king.

Because the Protectorate had relied on many trappings of monarchical culture, the Restoration was an easy transition. Yet the moral climate of Charles II's reign stood, again, in marked contrast to both the Protectorate and his father's reign. Throughout his exile, parliamentary propaganda had publicized Charles II's supposed sexual adventures in Paris: 'the gloating boast of Cromwellian propaganda credited the English "Tarquin" with the rape of every virtuous matron and the seduction of every helpless virgin within the arrondisements' (Kenyon 1982, p. 104). Even at his coronation, the sermon of George Morley, Bishop of Worcester, revealed 'that Charles' laziness and sexual indiscretions were already arousing the disapproval of many people in and close to the Court within the first year of his restoration' (Madway 2000, p. 146). Charles II's coronation reproduced, in its essentials, his father's coronation, but the restored king also made greater use of public festivities than had his father. This implied a greater accessibility to the court than that granted by Charles I, who sought privacy. As Lorraine Madway (2000, p. 148) notes:

> Charles II made sure he did not repeat his father's mistakes. He was also astute enough to understand that these aspects of the coronation, particularly the procession, gave him the opportunity to display himself directly to his subjects without any interference from the Church regarding the form and content of his presentation.

However, the king's very public sexual liaisons – one need only read Pepys' diary to see that they were common knowledge – undermined the dignity provided by ceremonial: 'Too often he [Charles II] gave his subjects occasions to feel that the presentation of kingship was not a show of majesty but a spectacle of mockery' (Madway 2000, p. 154). Though Charles II was able to keep the notion of hereditary succession intact through the Exclusion Crisis, the aura of regal authority had been seriously tarnished by his sexual behaviour.

Visual arts and architecture

Cultural patronage greatly influenced the arts in the seventeenth century. The two most significant figures in painting and architecture prior to the civil wars are Sir Anthony Van Dyck and Inigo Jones. Both men's accomplishments are evident in the remainder of the century. Van Dyck had worked in the studio of the Flemish painter Peter Paul Rubens and followed his master to England. In 1620, Van Dyck was granted a pension by James I, but it was not until Charles I's reign that, after several years on the continent studying the masters, he would achieve greatness. The king doubled his pension and knighted him in 1633. Van Dyck painted not only Charles I and his family, but also many aristocratic patrons. His influence on painting was strong, as he vibrantly transformed the rather lifeless Tudor style that is still evident in Daniel Myten's portraits of James I and his court. The prime painters of the latter part of the century, particularly Lely and Cooper, clearly reveal the impact Van Dyck had on painting in England.

The second individual, Inigo Jones, had been designing masques for James I's Queen Anne from 1605. He became Surveyor to Prince Henry in 1610, and from 1615 to 1642 was Surveyor of the King's Works. Influenced by continental architecture, particularly the neo-classicism of Palladio, Jones' earliest extant designs were for the New Exchange in the Strand. From 1619 to 1622, Jones designed and built the Banqueting House at Whitehall and began work on the Queen's House at Greenwich for Anne, though this was not completed until 1635 for Henrietta Maria. He also designed the Queen's Chapel at St James' Palace for Henrietta Maria and planned a new Whitehall. As David Watkin (2001, p. 98) points out, however, Jones' designs and buildings were not influential in his own lifetime, 'they were regarded as an alien court taste by the majority of patrons and designers'. Through his masque designs, Jones' belief that 'architecture was the physical expression of a carefully constructed system of social and political values' is most evident (Howarth 1993, p. 68). Indeed, in the 1630s, 'Jones is observed fashioning the Surveyorship of the King's Works into an avowedly political office' (Howarth 1993, p. 68). Jones' buildings and designs served as the architectural extension of regal authority.

Critics argue that Jones' masque settings engage with political issues of the time, for example Ship Money and plans to rebuild London. Jones had some influence on building in the capital through the Commission for New Buildings instituted by James I to counteract urban sprawl (unlicensed builders were fined – creating conflict between the crown and the city in Charles I's reign as the licenses were seen as a form of 'extra-parliamentary taxation'). Jones' role here is, perhaps, evident in his set designs for Thomas Carew's masque, *Coelum Britannicum* ('The British Heavens', 1634), in which the opening classical ruins are transformed to a glorious city through the benevolent virtues of Charles I and Henrietta Maria, hybridized as 'Carlomaria'. No other architect would have such an impact until Sir Christopher Wren.

In 1663, Wren began his first public commission. He was appointed Surveyor-General of the King's Works in 1669 – retaining this position through the reigns of Charles II, James II and William III – and, in the aftermath of the Great Fire of London in 1666, became the prime architect under the Rebuilding Act of 1670.

Theatre

Aristocratic patronage had always been essential to the survival of theatre in early modern England, and a brief exposition of some important issues prior to 1603 will help establish the contexts for our period. In 1572, four years before James Burbage built the first permanent London theatre, simply named The Theatre, 'An Act for the Punishment of Vagabonds, and for Relief of the Poor and Impotent' (cited in Harrison 1956, p. 19) was proclaimed. The statute addressed the 'great outrages, to the high displeasure of Almighty God, and to the great annoy of the commonweal'. Included in the statute (which carried the penalty of whipping and being 'burnt through the gristle of the right ear with a hot iron of the compass of an inch about') were 'common players in interludes and minstrels, not belonging to any baron of this realm or towards any other honourable personage of greater degree'. 'An Act for the Punishment of Vagabonds' was periodically restated during Elizabeth I's reign and also during the reign of James I. It is often cited as an example of the low standing of stage players, but the distinction is there in the statute itself – players belonging to a 'baron', or indeed, the royal household, are exempt from its scope.

Patronage also assisted the theatres to survive anti-theatrical attacks from Puritans and concern from the London city authorities. In 1579, only three years after Burbage's Theatre opened, Stephen Gosson published the first major anti-theatrical work, *The School of Abuse*. Puritan anti-theatricality asserted not only that plays were presenting irreligious sentiments – including, of course, satirical representations of Puritans – but that they were also representative of the nation's moral decline. Many anti-theatricalists focused on the convention of the boy actor in female attire, usually drawing on the condemnation of cross-dressing in the Old Testament books of Deuteronomy and Leviticus. Puritan writers believed that inordinate sexual desires were aroused by such gender confusion. Anti-theatricalism would culminate with William Prynne's compendious exposition of the moral evils of plays and players in *Histriomastix: The Players Scourge or Actors Tragedy* (1633). Prynne, however, would extend his critique of theatre beyond the public playhouses and the Inns of Court (the legal schools in London where plays were often performed) to include the royal court. For this, he was pilloried and his ears were cut off.

The London city authorities also expressed their displeasure with the theatres on the grounds of immoral behaviour – presenting not only irreligious or seditious entertainment, but also because of the other forms of 'entertainment' with which the theatres were associated, including prostitution, gambling and bear- and bull-baiting. This is why playhouses were built in the suburbs, particularly Southwark, on the south bank of the Thames. This put them outside the city's jurisdiction, though it did not prevent periodic conflict between the city, the royal household and aristocratic patrons of the theatres. In a sense, these conflicts would be resolved shortly after the outbreak of the civil wars when Parliament ordered the theatres closed in September 1642. The buildings either fell into disrepair or were torn down; for example, the Globe was torn down in 1644, and the Fortune was pillaged in 1649 and destroyed in 1655.

But when James I acceded to the throne in 1603, aristocratic and royal patronage of the theatre was reconfigured. Most notable, of course, was the elevation of Shakespeare's company, the Lord Chamberlain's Men, to the King's Men in Letters Patent granted on 19 May 1603. The Letters Patent clearly address the opposition of Puritan anti-theatricalists and the London authorities:

> Willinge and Commundinge you and everie of you, as you tender our pleasure, not onelie to permitt and suffer them herein without anie your lettes hindrances or molestacions during our said pleasure.
>
> (cited in Greenblatt *et al.* 1997, p. 3335)

James I's attitude towards the theatre foreshadows the ideological import of his Declaration of Sports (1618). Other companies were aligned, or new ones formed, with members of the royal family: the Admiral's Men became Prince Henry's Men, passing to the patronage of his brother-in-law following the Prince of Wales' death; Worcester's Men became the Queen's Men, which dissolved upon Anne's death; a company under Princess Elizabeth's patronage was formed in 1611; and Prince Charles' Men, later the Prince of Wales' Men, was also founded. Royal patronage continued through Charles I's reign.

Within a month of the outbreak of civil war in 1642, however, the theatres were ordered closed by Parliament. They would not reopen until the Restoration. While the link between aristocratic patronage and the playhouses was re-established, the Restoration theatre was fundamentally different – influenced in large part by the exiled court's experience of French theatre. Restoration theatre companies were established by patent, rather than by theatrical entrepreneurs. There were two principal patent companies: one under the control of Sir William Davenant and the other under Thomas Killigrew. Davenant ran the Duke's Company, under the patronage of the king's brother James, Duke of York, at Dorset Garden, and Killigrew managed the King's Company at the Theatre Royal. In addition, each company was granted exclusive rights to a repertoire, and the King's Company had the best plays of the Elizabethan, Jacobean and Caroline periods. While at first this was a drawback for the Duke's Company – even Davenant had to petition for the Duke's Company to perform his own plays from earlier in the century – it encouraged the re-emergence of play writing as a craft after almost two decades. Indeed, the Duke's Company would supersede the King's and absorb it in 1682.

Another important change was the appearance of female actors. Prior to 1642, boy actors played female roles. As noted above, this convention had contributed to the ire of anti-theatricalists for, supposedly, arousing 'inordinate desires'. It was thought that female actors could improve the moral climate of the playhouses. Two points are noteworthy in regards to this development. First, there were still some male actors specializing in female roles, most notably Edward Kynaston. Pepys' comments on Kynaston are interesting. On 18 August 1660, Pepys (1960, p. 48) saw *The Loyal Subject*, and wrote in his diary: 'one Kinaston, a boy, acted the Duke's sister, but made the loveliest lady that ever I saw in my life, only her voice not very good'. Pepys (1960, p. 64) again saw Kynaston perform in an adaptation of Jonson's *The Silent Woman* on 7 January 1661:

> Among other things here, Kinaston, the boy, had the good turn to appear in three shapes; first as a poor woman in ordinary clothes, to please Morose; then in fine clothes as a gallant, and in them was clearly the prettiest woman in the whole house; and lastly as a man, and then likewise did appear the handsomest man in the house.

Pepys' comments on Kynaston as a lovely or pretty lady curiously support the concerns of gender confusion that obsessed earlier anti-theatricalists. The second point is that female actors could not escape gender stereotypes. By performing in public, they were often seen as 'whores' in an equation which linked public display with sexual availability in the minds of contemporaries.

Along with changes in the operation of the theatres and the introduction of female actors, there were also architectural changes. Rather than the old, outdoor round theatres of the pre-civil war years, Dorset Garden and the Theatre Royal were indoor theatres, modelled on the French theatres frequented by Charles II's exiled court. The proscenium stage was used, while artificial lighting and stage machinery allowed for increasingly spectacular sets. The Restoration stage, in fact, became dominated by spectacle. Seating, too, was restructured. While theatre seating arrangements had always reflected the social hierarchy, the Restoration playhouses marked this off much more clearly. The pit was the cheaper, popular seating area, with more expensive box-seating and galleries. The playhouses came to be patronized by a more exclusive, upper-class audience, and it would be their tastes – a development which began when the indoor theatre of Blackfriars had served as the principal theatre for the King's Men earlier in the century – that would determine the repertoire.

Censorship and print

Press censorship during the period is known as licensing – a form of pre-publication censorship. Licensing had existed in England since Henry VIII's time (both pre- and post-Reformation). Efforts to enforce licensing were not always stringent, nor were they entirely effective. All manuscripts (even imported books and reprints) were required to be examined by an ecclesiastical censor (the office of the Bishop of London) and political censors. In addition, all publications required the examiner's and the printer's name.

The printers' guild, the Stationers' Company, was also bound to aid in the enforcement of the law – although their compliance was most certainly in their own economic interests. Henry VIII's licensing regulations were affirmed by succeeding monarchs through to James I. In 1637, however, Charles I tightened these controls: the Star Chamber Decree required all publications to be entered in the Stationers' Register and stipulated that the examiner's imprimatur, as well as the names of both author and printer be on the title page. It also limited the number of master printers and presses, providing the Stationers' Company with the right of search and seizure.

With the abolition of the much-hated Court of Star Chamber in 1641, Parliament seems to have been oblivious to the consequences relating to print. Printers sprang up in the capital, and publications flowed from their presses. Parliament attempted to regain control, but it was not until the Licensing Order of 1643 that a concerted effort to regulate printing was again put in place. The Licensing Order – which John Milton argued against in *Areopagitica* (1643) – essentially re-established the press controls of the Star Chamber Decree of 1637, and these principles would be periodically reaffirmed by Parliament through to 1655, largely in an effort to curb the growth of radical religious sects and political groups who took advantage of the press to present their ideas to the reading public. Somewhat ironically, Milton served as a licenser in the early 1650s. Another attempt to impose an effective form of censorship followed the Restoration. In 1663, Roger L'Estrange (Royalist plotter through the 1640s and 1650s and, in the Restoration, editor of a newsbook) attracted the attention of Charles II by writing *Considerations and Proposals in Order to the Regulation of the Press*. This soon after earned him the position of Surveyor of the Imprimery and Printing Presses, which he held until 1688.

But it was not only radical religious sects and political groups which took advantage of print; royalists also benefited from ineffectual attempts at press censorship. The most notable example is the publication, on the day of his execution, of Charles I's *Eikon Basilike* (1649) – the king's self-justification of his actions from 1640 through the civil wars, though the book is now attributed to his chaplain, John Gauden. The publication of Cavalier verse by the most prominent royalist publisher, Humphrey Moseley, also served Charles I's cause and kept it alive through the Interregnum. For example, the title pages of Moseley's editions of Thomas Carew's and Sir John Suckling's work through the 1640s and 1650s mark a sense of loss of the Caroline Golden Age. Within the polemical struggle being fought out in print in the 1640s and 1650s, the publication of their work was a defiant, political act by Moseley and other royalist printers.

POLITICS AND RELIGION

Politics

King and Parliament
The relationship between the king and Parliament (consisting of Lords and Commons) was, even at the best of times, strained for the four Stuart monarchs of our period: James I (1603–25), Charles I (1625–49), Charles II (1660–85) and James II (1685–88). Parliament, with the exception of the civil-war period and the Interregnum, was only called at the monarch's pleasure, usually when he required money beyond the ordinary revenues allotted for his expenses. The traditional model of the monarch living off this income during times of peace, however, was becoming increasingly untenable in the seventeenth century. The financial expedients open to the monarch were selling crown lands, granting monopolies, farming the customs and selling titles. All of these methods were only viable for a short term. In addition, these methods of raising money also tended to weaken the very institution of monarchy by eroding future financial stability. Any additional money had to be obtained through Parliament but, in return for this, the monarch was expected

to hear his subjects' grievances and provide some redress. This political process often led to conflict, resulting in Parliament attempting to assert its privileges and the monarch claiming royal prerogative. Such debates centred on the appointment of royal counsellors; the education and marriage of the royal children; war; foreign policy; finances; and, later in the century, the succession itself. Each of these political matters were intensely intertwined with religious issues and the battle over defining England as a Protestant nation.

Conflict between Parliament and the monarch could develop beyond heated verbal exchanges. Parliament did, on occasion, attempt to impeach royal counsellors that it singled out as responsible for the kingdom's woes: the Duke of Buckingham in 1626, the Earl of Strafford in 1640 and the Earl of Clarendon in 1667. Buckingham's impeachment failed, while Strafford and Clarendon were sacrificed by their respective kings in an attempt to placate political tensions. The result of such clashes generally ended with the monarch either proroguing or dissolving Parliament. In extreme instances, the leaders of parliamentary opposition to royal policy could be arrested. It is also important to note that party politics as we know it did not emerge until the reign of Charles II. These parties aligned themselves with either the rights of Parliament (Whig) or the monarch (Tory). However, the prorogation or dissolution of Parliament by the king left him without any additional funds. This forced him to fall back on the expedients cited above to raise money. In some cases, the monarch would take extraordinary measures to meet his financial requirements. For example, Charles I dissolved Parliament in 1629 and began the 'eleven years of personal rule'. He instituted extra-parliamentary forms of taxation, most of these based on the reassertion of the monarch's older feudal rights. But the most hated of these was the collection of Ship Money beginning in 1634. This tax, used in times of war to support the navy by taxing coastal towns, was extended in peace by Charles I to inland towns. Another means of avoiding Parliament was utilized by

Charles II. In 1670, he entered into the Treaty of Dover with Louis XIV of France, which provided Charles II with a secret annual subsidy. In both cases, however, these extraordinary measures did not succeed in freeing the monarch from having to call Parliament over the long run. In Charles I's case, the 'eleven years of personal rule' came to a devastating conclusion following the two Bishops' Wars with Scotland when he was forced to call Parliament in 1640 – first the Short and then the Long Parliament.

Civil Wars and the execution of Charles I

The Long Parliament quickly asserted its rights – impeaching the Earl of Strafford as an 'evil' counsellor, and passing important legislation which prevented its dissolution without its consent. In addition, the Grand Remonstrance, passed by Parliament on 23 November 1641, explicitly laid out the failings of Charles I's government in 204 articles. The reading of the Remonstrance coincided with the arrival of news in London that rebellion had broken out in predominantly Catholic Ireland. Fearing that the king may treat with the Irish rebels in order to bring an Irish-Catholic army into England to pacify parliamentary opposition, Parliament moved to strip Charles I of control of the militia.

The king's failed attempt to arrest the parliamentary leaders in January 1642 only served to strengthen the more extreme elements in Parliament as well as solidify popular support for them in the capital. With the political situation worsening in London, Charles I left the capital early in 1642, headed north to rally support for his cause, and raised his standard at Nottingham on 22 August 1642. The first engagement of the civil war occurred at Edgehill two months later. The battle was a stalemate and, as such, it set the tone of the military conflict for the next two and a half years. Parliament's proposals to end the conflict, from 1642 right through until late in 1648, were consistently rejected by Charles as challenges to his prerogative. It became clear to both the king and Parliament that outside assistance would be required to bring about a decisive victory – Charles looked to both the Continent and Ireland, while Parliament looked to the Scots.

Parliament would achieve an alliance first. In September 1643, the Solemn League and Covenant was agreed upon with the Scots. It would have significant long-reaching consequences. In return for Scots' military support, Parliament agreed to reform the Church along Presbyterian lines; extirpate Catholicism and radical Protestant sects; bring 'incendiaries, malignants, and evil instruments' to justice; defend the rights and liberties of Parliament; and, what would become the most contentious issue, 'preserve and defend the King's Majesty's person and authority' (Gardiner 1951, pp. 268–70). The Solemn League and Covenant would create a Presbyterian ascendancy in Parliament for the next few years, which continually asserted the principles of the agreement. While the Covenant created a joint military force with the potential to defeat Charles decisively, the stipulation to preserve the king's person and authority exacerbated a rift in Parliament that developed into war and peace parties. Those MPs who desired a more aggressive policy with the intention of breaking the stalemate on the battlefield, in order to achieve a clear-cut military defeat of the king, came to the fore and proceeded to make plans to restructure Parliament's armies into a centralized command. These debates led to the creation of the New Model Army early in 1645. The New Model Army's first test came at Naseby on 14 June of that year – and it passed with a resounding victory. The battle was the turning point of the first civil war, as the king could not recover from the material losses he suffered.

However, the potential of success on the battlefield did nothing to unify Parliament. As long as the king had presented a threat to the rights and liberties of the subject (as represented by Parliament), differences amongst parliamentarians could be accommodated. Now, Presbyterian dominance in Parliament was beginning to face a significant challenge from the Independents, who desired greater religious toleration (barring Catholicism). But the first civil war would end with neither a last decisive battle nor a negotiated settlement. Perhaps attempting to take advantage of the divisions in Parliament, Charles, disguised as a servant, turned himself over to Scots' headquarters at Newark in May 1646. There, Charles negotiated separately with both the Scots and Parliament, eventually accepting neither party's offers. Frustrated with the king, the Scots negotiated with Parliament to withdraw their troops from England in return for £400,000 and handed Charles over to parliamentary custody in January 1647.

It was within this context that the Army stepped forward as a political force. In March 1647, many regiments began to demand their arrears of pay and resisted impressment for the Irish expedition that had been long delayed by the civil war. Regiments selected 'agitators', basically spokesmen to present their grievances, and a Council of the Army was established, challenging Parliament's authority. In May, New Model Army regiments refused Parliament's order to disband, demanding that their grievances first be addressed. Then, on 3 June, Coronet Joyce, without the approval but most certainly with the knowledge of senior officers, arrived at Holmby House, where Parliament held the king. Joyce requested that Charles accompany him to Army headquarters, and the king, seeing another opportunity to divide and conquer, obliged. The Army now had the most significant bargaining tool with which to challenge Parliament's authority. Indeed, in July, the Army presented its grievances to Parliament in the *Heads of the Proposals*. Civil unrest exploded in the capital. Parliament was stormed by a mob and approximately 100 MPs fled London, appealing to Lord General Thomas Fairfax for protection. On 3 August, the New Model Army entered London and restored order.

As in Parliament, there were now significant divisions within the army. The rank and file were heavily influenced by the more democratic ideals of the Levellers, even to the point of criticizing senior officers as 'grandees'. Tensions within the army led to the Putney Debates between senior officers and the Levellers in October 1647. These were highly charged meetings, as a conservative reaction in regards to property came to the fore. Faced with a challenge to their authority, and mutiny, the senior officers ordered the Army to winter quarters.

Meanwhile, Charles continued to treat with both the Scots and Parliament, accepting, in December 1647, the Scots' Engagement. With the promise of the Scots' military support for the king, the realm was on course for a second civil war. Parliament broke off all negotiations with Charles, alarmed by both the growing popular resentment to the military apparatus and royalist uprisings. The Scots invasion, however, was delayed and therefore unable to take advantage of these events. When it did cross the border into England, the Scots army was crushed at Preston on 17 August 1648. Parliament was now trapped between a radicalized New Model Army and a recalcitrant king, prompting it to make one last attempt to negotiate with Charles. The Army, however, had hardened its position, and, while it waited to learn of the result of the negotiations between Parliament and the king, it prepared its own solution. Upon Parliament's failure to arrive at a settlement with Charles, the Army presented it with the *Army Remonstrance* on 20 November, and quickly followed this with Colonel Pride's purge of Parliament on 6 December (which removed nearly half of the MPs, primarily Presbyterians, and created the Rump). This paved the way for the trial of Charles I for 'high and treasonable offences' (Gardiner 1951, p. 357), resulting in his execution on 30 January 1649.

Political experimentation: Commonwealth and Protectorate

The monarchical body politic analogy – that the king was the rational head of the kingdom – was literally split asunder with Charles' beheading. The Rump Parliament then set about attempting to restructure political allegiance. It was neither an easy, nor entirely successful, process. The Rump appointed a Council of State, abolished the monarchy and the House of Lords and declared England a 'Commonwealth and Free State'. But none of this had a particularly radical import, as their goal remained an essentially conservative one: the protection of property, hierarchy and, though somewhat paradoxical in regards to the execution of the king, patriarchy. Opposition remained from royalists, Presbyterians, religious sects and the Levellers, of course. The Army, too, still had its own problems. The influence of Leveller ideals amongst the rank and file prompted continued resistance to impressment for service in Ireland and demands for arrears of pay. Mutinies occurred in the spring of 1649, with a number of soldiers being executed as examples before discipline could be restored. With the mutinies put down, the Commonwealth quickly swung into military action. Cromwell personally commanded the long-delayed Irish expedition and brutally reasserted English rights in Ireland. While the Irish threat was being resolved, a plan to restore Charles II was brewing in Scotland. In 1650, Charles II agreed to the Covenant in order to gain Scottish military support. In response, Cromwell crossed the Tweed in July and won a crushing victory at Dunbar on 3 September 1650. As Cromwell's troops occupied Edinburgh and Glasgow, Charles II and his allies, hoping for support from royalist uprisings in England, made a dash across the border; however, on 3 September 1651, this force was routed at Worcester by Cromwell. Charles escaped to France, where he would remain until 1660. The Celtic periphery – Scotland, where Charles I's troubles had begun and the possible royalist base of Ireland – had been secured for the Commonwealth.

But the execution of the king had not solved the political dilemma in England. Indeed, the troubled relationship between monarch and Parliament in previous decades would be replayed between Cromwell and Parliament. The Rump accomplished little in the way of legislation, and the continued growth of the religious sects also contributed to this problem. Cromwell dissolved the Rump on 22 April 1653, prompting a debate on a suitable form of government – including the offer of the crown to Cromwell. The offer was declined, twice, with Cromwell accepting the title of Protector. Problems with legislative authority also coincided with increasing popular opposition to the regime. This was further exacerbated by the appointment in the localities of major-generals whose daunting presence, it was hoped, would maintain order. There was so much local opposition to the major-generals, however, that their reigns lasted barely a year. But the Army's role in politics would remain and shortly made itself apparent following the death of Oliver Cromwell on 3 September 1658. Oliver had named his son Richard successor, curiously following primogeniture by choosing his eldest son, with no political experience, over his younger son, Henry, an able military commander in Ireland. Though the Army expressed its loyalty to the new Protector, Richard's time was short, and marked by a dizzying cycle of Parliaments. With unrest growing, General Monck, military governor of Scotland, who had served first the king and then Parliament during the civil wars, began to march south to London. On 11 February 1660, Monck dissolved the Rump and recalled the Long Parliament, which quickly appointed Monck Lord General and set a date for elections before dissolving itself. The new Convention Parliament restored the House of Lords, with the exception of the bishops, and declared that the Government consisted of the king, Lords and Commons.

On the Continent, Charles II could not be more pleased. At Monck's request, Charles issued the Declaration of Breda on 4 April 1660, granting a general pardon and expressing the king's willingness to work with Parliament to reach a political settlement and pay the army's arrears. No other significant political concessions were asked of Charles II, and, on 1 May, the resolution to restore the monarchy passed both Houses.

Religion

King, Parliament and Puritans

It is important to remember that 'Puritan' was a derogatory term applied to moderate and a small minority of radical reformers. Calls for reform centred around the excision of rites, ceremonies and episcopacy retained by the Elizabethan religious settlement which James I inherited. These were seen by Puritans as evidence that the Reformation begun by Henry VIII had never been fully realized. There was no major theological disagreement: the established Church and its hierarchy, the king and the reformers were orthodox Calvinists, and 'contemporaries would have found any suggestion that Calvinists were Puritans completely incomprehensible' (Tyacke 1978, p. 120). Those seeking religious reform were hopeful that James I, having reigned in a predominately Presbyterian Scotland prior to his accession to the English throne, would heed their calls, and they moved quickly to present their case. On his progress south to London in 1603, the king was presented with the Millenary Petition. The petition called for a 'godly reformation' of the Church, focusing on rites and ceremonies deemed to be insupportable by Scripture and the result of centuries of Catholic corruption. The petitioners also asked James for the opportunity to present their case before him more fully. Always interested in disputation, James established the Hampton Court Conference, which convened on 14 January 1604 and sat for three days. While the Anglican hierarchy was initially uncertain about the firmness of the king's belief in episcopacy, the conference demonstrated James' desire to maintain royal control of the Church. James enthusiastically engaged with the debates at first and seemed willing to accept that some moderate reforms were needed, but it quickly became clear that the king would not accept the petitioners' more radical views of 'godly reformation'. On the second day of the conference, for example, James attacked a scheme for reorganizing the hierarchical Church by denouncing the suggestion as 'aymed at a *Scottish Presbytery*, which . . . as well agreeth with a monarchy as God and the Devil' (Ashton 1969, p. 183). The exchange prompted the oft-quoted dictum from James, 'No Bishop, no King'.

The Hampton Court Conference led to a new Prayer Book and a new set of Canons in 1604. The reforms raised at the conference that the king and Church hierarchy were uninterested in were simply forgotten. In addition, Richard Bancroft, Archbishop of Canterbury, set about removing the small minority of non-conformist clergymen from their livings. Perhaps the most significant outcome of the Hampton Court Conference was the project of proceeding with an authorized English translation of the Bible. The King James Authorized Bible, published in 1611, was carefully translated by appointees and, importantly, vetted and approved by the Church hierarchy before receiving royal approval. The finished project is a monument of the English language.

But a significant shift in church policy occurred during the reign of Charles I, and in 1629, Parliament mounted a strenuous attack on Arminianism. Named after the Dutch theologian Jacob Arminius (who, incidentally, was initially employed to defend Calvinism), Arminianism essentially expunged or, at the very least, alleviated the strict predestination theology of Calvinism by reintroducing a role for free will. James I had provided no preferment for clergymen of Arminian beliefs. The most notable example of the change under Charles I is that of William Laud. Laud did not move far up the hierarchy during James I's reign. Created a royal chaplain in 1611, he was eventually given the living of the small Welsh see of St David's in 1621. In 1626, however, he received the bishopric of Bath and Wells, followed in 1628 by London and, in 1633, the archbishopric of Canterbury. Now, throughout the Church, Arminian clergymen were shown favour and Church ritual was formalized. Parliament's grievances against Arminianism were linked to the ongoing attacks on rites and ceremonies, coupled with anti-Catholicism which was spurred by the queen's adherence to the Roman faith. Fears of Henrietta Maria's influence over the king, as well as high-profile court conversions, which Charles did not prevent (though he did not endorse them), also contributed to religious tensions.

Although faced with both political and religious opposition in England, a more significant threat to Charles I's authority would develop in Scotland. In 1633, Charles travelled north for his belated Scots coronation. He returned to England determined to impose uniformity, and his authority, on the Scots Kirk. Along with Laud, Charles planned to install episcopacy, new canons and the Prayer Book. These plans met with significant opposition, including rioting in Edinburgh. The Scottish Privy Council was left with no option but to suspend the enforcement of the new canons and the Prayer Book. The creation of the Scots' National Covenant followed in response to the attempt to impose such unwanted, 'popish' innovations on the Kirk. While Charles sent a representative to Edinburgh to negotiate with the Covenanters, he also put England on a war footing. The king's intransigence led to the two Bishops' Wars with Scotland and his need, in the face of military defeat, to convene the Short Parliament and, almost immediately afterwards, the Long Parliament in 1640.

The Long Parliament's political and religious grievances were closely linked. While proceedings against the Earl of Strafford were underway, Parliament was presented with a petition from the citizens of London and several counties requesting that episcopacy, 'with all its dependencies, roots and branches, may be abolished' (Gardiner 1951, p. 137). The Root and Branch Petition restated and elaborated on the religious grievances of the Millenary Petition and the Scots' National Covenant. But the Root and Branch Petition entered into very different political circumstances. For Parliament, the petition was an opportunity for using the presence of the Scots' army still in the north of England, since the end of the second Bishops' War, as a political lever, linking the religious grievances of the Root and Branch Petition to those of the Covenant. Indeed, the petition would lead to legislation with wide-ranging consequences. Parliament passed legislation to abolish the prerogative courts of Star Chamber and High Commission in July 1641 – courts which had, at times, dealt savagely with both religious and political dissidents. Legislation specifically affecting church reform was also passed, and bishops were excluded from the House of Lords. For many, it seemed as if the Reformation could finally be completed, although this euphoria was quickly dissipated and never regained with the rise of the radical religious sects during the Commonwealth and Protectorate.

Charles II's first parliament would move in the early years of the Restoration to reassert the authority of the Church of England and stamp out religious dissent. In part, the religious legislation of the Cavalier Parliament responded to the perceived threat posed by dissenters, particularly of the remnants of the more radical sects that had developed in the past two decades. It should also be noted that the Presbyterians largely acquiesced to the Restoration. Charles II had called the Savoy Conference in 1661 to bring together Episcopalians and Presbyterians – some Presbyterians even accepted bishoprics. From 1661 to 1664, however, religious reconciliation was not the intention of the majority of MPs. First, Parliament passed the Corporation Act (1661), which imposed oaths of supremacy and allegiance, along with a repudiation of the Solemn League and Covenant, on those holding civil office in order to remove former Cromwellians from their posts. The Act of Uniformity (1662) imposed these oaths on the clergy, along with acceptance of the Prayer Book, the Thirty-Nine Articles and ordination by a bishop. And, in 1664, the Conventicle Act banned all services other than those of the Church of England. These acts mark the change in nomenclature from Puritan to Dissenter. The religious legislation has come to be known as the Clarendon Code after Charles II's Lord Chancellor, Edward Hyde, Earl of Clarendon. Both Clarendon and the king, however, largely opposed this legislation. In fact, Charles issued Declarations of Indulgence, benefiting both Roman Catholics and Dissenters, in an attempt to temper these acts.

Civil wars and Interregnum: The rise of radical religious sects

The Presbyterian ascendance in Parliament was strengthened by the Solemn League and Covenant. The Scots now not only provided military support for Parliament's cause; they also contributed members to the Westminster Assembly of Divines (created in 1643), which was to oversee church reform in line with the terms of the Covenant. The Westminster Assembly progressively dismantled episcopacy, eventually abolishing it in 1646; established a Presbyterian church system; and replaced the Prayer Book with a Presbyterian Directory of Worship. The Presbyterians were not particularly tolerant of religious sectarianism, the most interesting literary example of this is Thomas Edwards' encyclopaedic *Gangraena: or a Catalogue and Discovery of Many of the Errours, Heresies, Blasphemies, and Pernicious Practices of the Sectaries of this Time* (1646). But following the creation of the New Model Army and its victory at the Battle of Naseby in the summer of 1645, power in Parliament shifted from the Presbyterians to the Independents. They desired an independent church structure, put more emphasis on the individual conscience of the believer and called for greater religious toleration (barring Catholicism). Hence, the differences between the Presbyterians and Independents in Parliament were both religious and political – and these would be exacerbated by the Covenant's stipulation to protect the king's majesty. The Presbyterians would eventually lose this conflict, as it culminated in the exclusion of Presbyterian members of Parliament in Pride's Purge, clearing the way for Charles I's trial and execution and the creation of the Commonwealth.

While the monarch and Parliament had a troubled relationship in previous decades, the execution of the king did not solve either the political or religious dilemmas the Commonwealth now faced. The Rump accomplished very little in the way of religious reform. Acts were passed barring clergymen from sitting in Parliament, abolishing compulsory church attendance and dealing with moral offences. These measures were necessary, as the abolition of the ecclesiastical courts removed the legal apparatus for dealing with such matters. The two most notable acts here were the Adultery Act and the Blasphemy Act, both of 1650. By the first, adultery was made a capital offense (incidentally, the only adulterers executed were four women), while the Blasphemy Act dealt with something much more tangible in terms of dangers to the social order. The decided conservative aim of the Blasphemy Act was meant to address the proliferation of sects over the past decade. These had flourished in a context where worldly authority had been rhetorically and violently contested. The sects had also benefited from the lapse in censorship laws following the abolition of both the court of Star Chamber and the ecclesiastical courts in 1641, along with the never entirely successful attempts by Parliament to reinstitute an effective censorship. The religious sects ranged from Quakers and Baptists to Ranters and Fifth Monarchists. In addition, the proto-communist Diggers, led by Gerrard Winstanley, were viewed with some trepidation. Though not strictly a religious sect, their agrarian, communal ideals were certainly indebted to the Bible. The Diggers began to cultivate wastelands in 1649 and were harassed, attacked and driven off the land by local magnates.

It is difficult to ascertain how widespread the most radical sects were, yet Ranters and Fifth Monarchists were clearly viewed as a great threat. The Ranters were antinomians, believing that divine grace rendered obedience to God's laws and the laws of the land unnecessary. Contemporaries represented the Ranters as openly sinning and committing acts of vice in order to, paradoxically, affirm their election. The Fifth Monarchists, on the other hand, wished to bring about Christ's reign on earth through armed rebellion. Sporadic Fifth Monarchist risings – and supposedly discovered plots – occurred in the 1640s and 1650s. These incidents involved only small groups of individuals, but the occurrence and fear of such rebellions, however intangible they may have been, hindered any attempts to further religious reformation. In part, the continued growth of religious sects contributed to Cromwell's dissolution of the Rump Parliament in 1653.

The last Fifth Monarchist incident, Venner's Rising, occurred in January 1661. It involved no more than three dozen armed rebels and was quickly put down. While the rising lasted sporadically for three days, and the heads of

14 rebels were placed upon spikes on London Bridge, the government feared something much larger was afoot. Order was restored by:

> a royal proclamation forbidding unauthorised meetings for any purpose and by directives to the militia to arrest all suspected persons and search houses. For those men who wished to persecute separatist groups and former republicans, a dream had come true.
>
> (Hutton 1987, p. 151)

Indeed, the Quakers suffered most from this crackdown on religious dissent, and it was in response to this persecution that the Quaker Peace Testimony originated.

Anti-Catholicism, politics and the Glorious Revolution

Anti-Catholicism played a part in political and religious debates of the period. In 1605, the Gunpowder Plot, a conspiracy by some Catholics to blow up both Parliament and the king, was discovered. The plot stirred an always present anti-Catholicism in the realm, particularly in Parliament. Immediately following the Gunpowder Plot, James did support calls for stricter enforcement of statutes against Catholics, though his policy in this regard gradually relaxed to a practical toleration of a peaceful Catholic laity, much to Parliament's consternation. Royal marriages to Catholics were also a contentious point of debate in Parliament: for example, Charles I to the French Henrietta Maria and James II to the Italian Mary of Modena. So, too, were foreign treaties with Catholic nations. Parliament feared that the heir to the throne would be brought up in the Catholic faith. The spectre of a Catholic succession rose to fever pitch during the Restoration because Charles II had no legitimate heir. Nor would the king choose either of the options open to him to ensure a Protestant succession: legitimize his eldest son, the Duke of Monmouth, or divorce his wife. The attitude of the Whigs in Parliament was also spurred by the public announcement of the conversion of James, Duke of York, to

Catholicism in 1673. As the king's eldest brother, James was the apparent successor to the throne. The link between Catholicism and tyrannical absolutism (or, as they termed it, 'arbitrary government') in the English political imagination threw the capital into a frenzy. In 1678, these tensions were fueled by Titus Oates' claim of a Catholic conspiracy to assassinate the king. The details of the Popish Plot provided by Oates were absurd, and he was himself a rather dubious character. But the coincidence of religious and political events, combined with the mysterious death of the magistrate who had originally taken Oates' deposition, made a potently volatile mix. In turn, Parliament called for stricter enforcement of recusancy laws and passed a second Test Act to bar Catholics from office, resulting in James, Duke of York's resignation from the Admiralty. The Exclusion Crisis was on, but the attempts of Whig members of Parliament to dictate the succession by excluding James and championing Monmouth were unsuccessful in the final years of Charles II's reign.

While James II's reign was short, he acceded peacefully to the throne. There was some reassurance in the fact that the succession would pass to James' Protestant daughter, Mary, and her husband, William of Orange. Even a 1685 rebellion by the disgruntled Monmouth, exiled by his father to the Netherlands in 1683, did not shake the Catholic king from his throne. But James II gradually alienated both Parliament and the Church of England through his pro-Catholic policies. For example, he unsuccessfully attempted to have the Test Act repealed – although James II did win a legal victory in 1686 allowing him to dispense with the Test Act in individual cases at his discretion. He also issued Declarations of Indulgence favourable to both Catholics and Dissenters.

All of the anxieties raised by these policies came to a head with the announcement at the end of 1687 that the Queen was pregnant – a potential Catholic heir which would displace Mary and William. James II reissued his Declaration of Indulgence favourable to Catholicism in April 1688, and the birth of James Francis Edward Stuart – who would later become known as the 'Old Pretender' – brought the situation to a head. In June 1688, Parliament 'invited' William 'to come to England and investigate the circumstances of the birth of the Prince of Wales and the condition of English liberties' (Kishlansky 1996, p. 277). But, from the time of the announcement of Mary of Modena's pregnancy, William had been planning an invasion to protect his claim to the Stuart throne. He landed at Torbay on 5 November 1688 (incidentally, the 83rd anniversary of the Gunpowder Plot). While William did not initially garner the support he had expected upon his arrival in England, James' support withered and he escaped to France.

William entered the capital and summoned a Convention to resolve the political crisis regarding the status of the anointed king, James II. Two options resulted: first, William and Mary could be declared regents during the life of James II, as the king had not officially abdicated. The second option resulted from William's rejection of the first. Only when he threatened to return to the Netherlands did the Convention resolve to declare William and Mary king and queen. They were crowned in April 1689 – a coronation which was also a victory for Parliament in its long-running debate with the monarch that it had a right to confirm the succession. Indeed, the Bill of Rights (1689) wrote James II and his son out of the succession – a clause which still prevents a Catholic from acceding to the throne. While the political situation in England was resolved, James II's only attempt to regain his crown began in Ireland in 1690. However, he was soundly defeated by William's forces at the Battle of the Boyne, leading to the Protestant ascendancy in Ireland and much more trouble to come.

SCIENCE AND PHILOSOPHY

The challenge to scholasticism

As the breakdown in political authority discussed in the previous section has demonstrated, men and women in the seventeenth century no longer unquestionably accepted age-old theories of social order. Their world was changing, and intellectual trends of the period reflect this. Developments in science and philosophy in the period are, broadly, attributable to a rejection of scholasticism which had long dominated education at both the grammar school and university levels. Scholasticism asserted the authority of the ancient canonical texts – the works of Aristotle, the Bible, and the Church fathers, for example. These texts were accorded the status of near infallibility and, therefore, were not to be questioned. Scientific and philosophical arguments were measured against this canon, and arguments were accepted, or 'proven', by citing authoritatively from these works: 'the "truth" of any proposition thus depended ultimately, not upon its corre-spondence with any particular "state of affairs", but upon its being consistent with a body of *given* and of course unques-tionable doctrine' (Willey 1953, p. 22). The new philosophy and science that emerged presented a significant challenge to these standards of knowledge, learning and authority. The questions posed by these intellectual developments led to new 'truths' about the world, and these 'truths' contributed to debates on the structure of the social order.

In science, the significance of the challenge to scholasti-cism resulted from experience and direct observation of the universe (empiricism) and, often, a self-conscious doubt of the possibility of attaining to knowledge through sensual per-ception (scepticism). The development of the telescope and microscope, for example, allowed human observers to see what had never been seen before by providing instrumental extensions of sensual perception. This affected the under-standing of both the cosmos and the human body. The work of astronomers such as Galileo, Copernicus and Kepler seri-ously questioned the model of the cosmos posited by Ptolemy, a second-century Alexandrian astrologer. Ptolemy's views were slightly revised over the centuries, but remained widely accepted until the sixteenth century. The earth was at the centre of the Ptolemaic universe, and it was surrounded by between nine and eleven concentric spheres increasing in diameter through the planetary spheres to that of the fixed stars and, finally, the *primum mobile* (the prime mover), which had been set in motion by God and controlled the motion of all of the spheres. Within this model of the cosmos, everything was comprised of four elements – earth, air, fire and water. Beneath the sphere of the moon, these four elements were mixed imperfectly and, consequently, they were in constant conflict. Hence, in the sublunary region, decay, death and mutability stood in contrast to the immutability of the heavens above it. In E. M. W. Tillyard's (1972, p. 47) words: 'Far from being dignified and tending to an insolent anthropocentricity, the earth in the Ptolemaic system was the cesspool of the universe, the repository of its grossest dregs.' The imperfect constitution of the earth accorded with the Christian theological notions of sin, the Fall and death. These theories did not entirely disappear until the end of the seventeenth century, as is evident in the poignant poetic use made of them in the verse of Donne and Milton's *Paradise Lost.*

Astrology was also intertwined with medical knowledge. It was thought that the human body was influenced by the heavens and comprised of the same four elements which made up the cosmos. The essential link here was developed into the theory of humoural psychology:

> Man's physical life begins with food, and food is made up of the four elements. Food passes through the stomach to the liver, which is lord of the lowest of the three parts of the body. The liver converts the food it receives into four liquid substances, the humours, which are to the human body what the elements are to the common matter of the earth. Each humour has its own counterpart among the elements.
>
> (Tillyard 1972, p. 76)

The correspondence of elements and humours were: earth – melancholy; water – phlegm; air – blood; and fire – choler (Tillyard 1972, p. 76). The combination of the humours in one's body determined one's character (this theory plays a significant role in Ben Jonson's comedies). The study of anatomy dismantled these theories. The sixteenth-century Flemish anatomist Vesalius challenged the ancient anatomical theories of the second-century Greek physician Galen. Galen's work on human anatomy, like Ptolemy's cosmos, had been canonized by the scholastics. But rather than unquestionably accept the texts of Galen as authoritative, Vesalius practised human dissection, discovered significant errors in Galen's texts and published his findings accompanied by exquisite illustrations. In England, this work was furthered by William Harvey's physiological observations, particularly his enquiries into the circulation of the blood (published in 1628).

Witches

The crumbling of what we might today see as superstitious or occult beliefs is also evident in the case of witchcraft. Though belief in witches persisted because of the Biblical assertion of their existence (the last witchcraft trial occurred in England in 1717), sceptics came to question their abilities in individual cases. While James I had written a tract on witchcraft, *Demonologie* (1597), his certainty in their powers cooled later in life. Sir Thomas Browne and Elizabeth Cary, Viscountess Falkland also provide fascinating examples of scepticism regarding witches in the seventeenth century. Both had first-hand experience of witch trials. Browne (a medical doctor and author) sat in on a trial in Bury St Edmunds in 1664. Though he did not doubt the existence of witches, he wrote in his *Commonplace Book* (cited in Patrides 1977, p. 27):

> We are no way doubtfull that there are wiches butt have not been always satisfied in the application of their wichcrafts or whether the parties under such affliction suffered from such hands.

As a young girl, Cary (who later wrote the first extant tragedy by a female author) suggested to her father, a magistrate who was presiding over a case of witchcraft, to ask the terrified female accused whether she had 'bewitched to death Mr John Symondes of such a place (her uncle that was one of the standers-by)' (*Lady Falkland: Her Life* 1994, p. 186–7). The poor woman said that she had, and after Symondes stepped forward, the woman explained, to a now more receptive courtroom, the threats she received if she had not confessed to the charges made against her.

Sir Francis Bacon and the new science

The new science in England was furthered most effectively, in particular, through the work of Sir Francis Bacon. Though not a scientist, Bacon established a systematic scientific method that was both experimental and inductive (reasoning from particular instances to general laws). He sought a means to further the progress of humanity in order to attain the authority over nature which he believed properly belonged to it. Bacon argues in the *Novum Organum* (1939a, p. 34) that the sceptics' doubt in attaining knowledge through the senses could be overcome through a comprehensive method of observation and instruments developed to aid perception:

> For the holders of that doctrine [scepticism] assert simply that nothing can be known; I also assert that not much can be known in nature by the way which is now in use. But then they go on to destroy the authority of the senses and understanding; whereas I proceed to devise and supply helps for the same.

For Bacon, falsity and error, what he called Idols, must first be cleared away before the empirical and inductive method can proceed. Bacon identified four idols: Idols of the Tribe, which are part of human nature; Idols of the Cave, which are ascribed to the 'peculiar nature' of each individual's beliefs; Idols of the Marketplace, arising from social intercourse; and Idols of the Theatre, which develop from 'the various dogmas of philosophies'.

In sweeping aside the Idols, however, Bacon maintained one specific boundary which should not be crossed – the divine; and this issue would result in persistent debate throughout the seventeenth century. Science was meant to provide dominion over nature, but did not authorize dominion over God in nature. In *The Great Instauration*, Bacon (1939b, p. 12) argues that science would purify and purge the mind while permitting 'to faith that which is faith's'. Yet science did, indeed, have an effect on religious belief. The discoverable mathematical laws of creation in the work of Sir Isaac Newton later in the century, for example, tended to construct a mechanistic and impersonal universe. Some Christians recoiled from this view that made humanity a rather insignificant part of a clockwork machine that God had wound-up. Attempts were made to accommodate new knowledge and philosophy into religious belief in what is called rational theology, which accepted the sceptics' fallibility of the senses as a means of attaining truth and coming to God, but asserted certainty through the rational soul. This is evident in the work of both Anglican and Puritan writers. For example, in his sermon *Via Intelligentiae*, Jeremy Taylor (1990, p. 374) argues that 'our reason' must be 'raised up by the Spirit of Christ', for there is something beyond this world 'that human learning without the addition of the divine can never reach'.

Science gained official sanction with the chartering of the Royal Society in 1662. The work conducted under its auspices both established experimental procedures, which led to a number of important discoveries, and gradually professionalized the scientific disciplines which had been performed primarily by dedicated amateurs. The make-up of the Society was decidedly conservative. First, there were no female members: though it did permit the visit of an interested woman such as Margaret Cavendish, Duchess of Newcastle. Pepys (1960, p. 394), himself a member of the Royal Society, saw her as something of an eccentric observer:

> The Duchesse hath been a good, comely woman; but her dress so antick and her deportment so ordinary that I do not like her

at all, nor did I hear her say any thing that was worth hearing, but she was full of admiration.

While Pepys' masculine chauvinism describes her as an awed, unintelligent observer, Cavendish's writings demonstrate the potentially radical gender conclusions that could be drawn from the new science. In Cavendish's *The Blazing World* (1666), as in Aphra Behn's translation of Fontenelle's *Conversations on the Plurality of Worlds* (1686), the liberating possibilities of science and yet undiscovered worlds informs her proto-feminist writings. Secondly, the Royal Society avoided granting membership to those it felt were scandalous in their opinions, such as Thomas Hobbes, seen by many as an atheist. Indeed, as if responding to concerns of the relationship between faith and science, many of the Royal Society's members were clergymen, including its first historian, Thomas Sprat, later Bishop of Rochester.

Philosophy and political theory

Developments in science and philosophy had marked implications in the field of political theory. Through the latter half of the seventeenth century, in particular, new ideas regarding sovereignty clashed with, and then superseded, the older ideas of the monarch's divine right, his paternal dominion over his subjects and the royal prerogative. Early in the century, James I had made much of the paternal analogy of kingship. In *The True Law of Free Monarchies* (1598), for example, James (1996, p. 57) argues that:

> By the law of nature, the king becomes a natural father to all his lieges at his coronation. And as the father of his fatherly duty is bound to care for the nourishing, education, and virtuous government of his children even so is the king bound to care for all his subjects.

Similarly, Sir Robert Filmer, a staunch royalist, also fully spoused divine right, paternal kingship and royal prerogative. His political writings were mainly composed in the first half of the century, and his published works of the 1650s polemically engaged with both Thomas Hobbes and John Milton. Filmer's most significant work, *Patriarcha* (1680), was not published until the Restoration, during the political tensions of the Exclusion Crisis. In *Patriarcha*, he argued that kingship was an extension of the dominion over creation given by God to Adam and its perpetuation through the Old Testament patriarchs and on to monarchs, specifically tying divine right to paternal kingship.

But the greatest philosophical accomplishment of our period is Thomas Hobbes' *Leviathan, or The Matter, Forme, & Power of a Common-Wealth Ecclesiastical and Civill* (1651). Hobbes' view of humanity and the Commonwealth in this work demonstrates a brilliant mind engaged with the turmoil of the civil wars and their aftermath. *Leviathan* has been described as:

> the most radical portrayal, among all those which appeared during the revolutionary years in England, of the human individual existing at a moment of near-total disintegration and artificially recreating authority from a state of dereliction.
>
> (Pocock 2003, p. 380)

In relation to the challenges posed by science to religion and older patterns of belief and authority, *Leviathan* works toward a comprehensive theory of human behaviour and political society. Hobbes carefully proceeds in the first book to define his terms through an exposition of 'Man': comprising, for example, imagination, passions, the state of nature and religion. From there, he moves through the Commonwealth, the Christian Commonwealth and the Kingdom of Darkness.

Hobbes argues that in order to escape from the 'state of nature' – where the passions of individual humans prompt a perpetual state of war, making 'the life of man, solitary, poore, nasty, brutish, and short' (Hobbes 1988, p. 186) – human beings eventually realize a need to contract amongst themselves to create a power above them. They will then have an arbiter to settle their conflicts and their best interests will be preserved. This Hobbes (1988, p. 81) calls the Leviathan:

> Nature (the Art whereby God hath made and governes the World) is by the *Art* of man, as in many other things, so in this also imitated, that it can make an Artificial Animal . . . *Art* goes yet further, imitating that Rationall and most excellent worke of Nature, *Man*. For by Art is created that great LEVIATHAN called a COMMON-WEALTH, or STATE, (in latine CIVITAS) which is but an Artificiall Man.

Hobbes' stress on motion (related in particular to the passions that drive us) and rationality – the latter essential in attaining a science of politics – is in accord with the scientific revolution. His notion of the social contract also attempts to comprehend a much more stable political system in relation to the many debates through the 1640s, in particular, which attempted either to rediscover the original contract or to posit new theories of political allegiance challenging monarchical sovereignty. Christopher Hill (2001, pp. 249–50) identifies three key developments in the Hobbesian revolution: 'expediency, not morality, is . . . the motive for political obedience'; 'power, not right, [is] the key question in politics'; and 'reason, not authority, [is] the arbiter in politics'. It is a paradox, Hill remarks, that 'the absolutist Hobbes demonstrated that the state exists for man, that it is the product of human reason, and therefore that political theory is a rational science'.

In the latter part of our period, John Locke engaged with the political theories of both Filmer and Hobbes in his two *Treatises of Government* (1690). These works provided the theoretical justification for the Glorious Revolution of 1688. Locke challenged the notion of a king's 'paternal dominion', viewed royal prerogative as 'an arbitrary power to do things hurtful to the people' (Locke 1952, p. 93) and argued that Hobbes' 'state of nature' and the 'state of war' were not commensurate. Like Hobbes, Locke argued that human beings come together and consent to the creation of a 'politic society'. However, unlike Hobbes, this accomplishes more than simply self-preservation. Locke firmly associates liberty with property and enshrines these as rights that no one man (such as a king) can take from him without due process of law.

Science, philosophy and language

Philosophy and science also shared one other very significant concern: language. When commenting on the Idols of the Marketplace in the *Novum Organum*, Bacon (1939a, p. 35) states:

> For it is by discourse that men associate; and words are imposed according to the apprehension of the vulgar. And therefore the ill and unfit choice of words wonderfully obstructs the understanding. Nor do the definitions or explanations wherewith in some things learned men are wont to guard and defend themselves, by any means set the matter right. But words plainly force and overrule the understanding, and throw all into confusion, and lead men away into numberless empty controversies and idle fancies.

Similarly, Hobbes (1988, p. 109) is concerned with 'inconstant signification'. He argues that conflict and error could come about from language:

> in the right Definition of Names, lyes the first use of Speech; which is the Acquisition of Science: And in wrong, or no Definitions, lyes the first abuse; from which proceed all false and senslesse Tenets; which make those men that take their instruction from the authority of books, and not from their own meditation, to be as much below the condition of ignorant men, as men endued with true Science are above it.
>
> (1988, p. 106)

Rectifying a perceived imprecision in language would also preoccupy the Royal Society. Within two years of its founding, the Society established a commission to 'improve' the English language. They also chose to record their experiments in English, rather than Latin, the latter still considered the international language of learning. In his *History of the Royal Society of London*, Sprat (Rudrum *et al*. 2001b, p. 660) states that the Civil Wars had ushered in 'many fantastical terms, which were introduced by our religious sects; and many outlandish phrases'. Indeed, for Sprat (Rudrum *et al*. 2001b, p. 662), the settled, peaceful Restoration allowed the members of the Society to bring the language to 'its last perfection' by restoring to it:

> the primitive purity, and shortness, when men delivered so many things, almost in an equal number of words. They have exacted from all their members, a close, naked, natural way of speaking; positive expressions; clear senses; a native easiness: bringing all things as near the mathematical plainness, as they can: and preferring the language of artisans, countrymen, and merchants, before that of wits, or scholars.

The use of a 'mathematical plainness' of language is evident in a brief comparison of medical treatises of the period. The writings of the Royal Society – avoiding figurative language and working toward a precision in vocabulary – stand in marked contrast to works written in the first half of the century. For example, the playwright Thomas Dekker's account of the London plague of 1603 – *The Wonderfull Yeare. 1603. Wherein is Shewed a Picture of London Lying Sicke of the Plague* (1603) – is an allegorical tale of a personified plague stalking the city. Dekker's tract is similar to plague tracts such as Benjamin Spenser's *Vox Civitatis: or, London Complaint Against her Children in the Countrey* (1603); and George Wither's *Britain's Remembrancer containing a Narration of the Plague lately past; A Declaration of the Mischiefs Present; and a Prediction of Judgments to Come* (1628) – both Spenser and Wither rely on supernatural causes while allegorically linking the plague to moral decline. As medical knowledge had progressed through the middle of the century, accounts of the plague of

1665, while not entirely dropping the moral arguments, are much more recognizably scientific in their approach to, and comprehension of, disease.

In addition, the notions of language put forward by philosophers and the Royal Society were hostile to imaginative literature – in Sprat's categorization, the language of 'wits'. Hobbes (1988, pp. 116–17), for example, argues that 'Metaphors, and senslesse and ambiguous words, are like *ignes fatui*; and reasoning upon them, is wandering amongst innumerable absurdities; and their end, contention, and sedition, or contempt'. Such attitudes to language and its use provide a broad context for understanding the antipathy in the last part of the century to what has come to be known as Metaphysical verse. Dryden was a member of the Royal Society from its inception until 1666; he was also on the committee to improve the English language. In *An Essay on Dramatic Poesy* (1667), Dryden (1985, p. 38) singles out the poet and satirist John Cleveland as an example of earlier writers who were seen as 'wresting and torturing a word into another meaning'. Although one can find Metaphysical elements in Dryden's early work, scientific terminology comes to play a significant part in his poetic vocabulary (see, for example, *Annus Mirabilis* (1667)) – a marked change from Donne's alchemical imagery and from the hermeticism of Henry Vaughan, Dryden's contemporary. Interestingly, the poet singled out in the next century as exemplary of the Metaphysical school of poets by Samuel Johnson, Abraham Cowley (Rudrum *et al.* 2001a, p. 308), like Dryden a member of the Royal Society, shares these concerns regarding language. In his ode 'To the Royal Society', Cowley (Rudrum *et al.* 2001a, p. 308) asserts an important social role for the poet, who, like the scientist: 'The real object must command / Each Judgment of his Eye, and Motion of his Hand'.

2

Literature in the Seventeenth Century

MAJOR GENRES

Poetry

John Donne and the anti-Petrarchan lyric
Poetry of the seventeenth century, particularly the lyric, is marked by a serious questioning of literary conventions. There are two contributing factors: first, as in all periods, literary innovation developed to challenge clichéd conventions; second, political and religious upheaval, coupled with developments in science and philosophy, significantly affected how writers handled conventions in responding to their world. In the latter part of Elizabeth I's reign, for example, the sonnets of Sir Philip Sidney, Edmund Spenser and William Shakespeare challenged the limits of Petrarchan conventions as a means of representing desire. In the early Jacobean

period, Lady Mary Wroth's sonnet sequence, *Pamphilia to Amphilanthus* (published 1621), wonderfully reverses the ego-centric male Petrarchan tradition by appropriating his conventions for her female speaker. The shift away from Petrarchanism, however, is most pronounced in the poetry of John Donne and his Metaphysical followers.

Donne's verse was not published until 1633, and although much of his work was written in the 1590s (particularly his secular lyrics), his poetic influence and innovation is most strongly felt in our period. As Thomas Carew (Rudrum *et al.* 2001a, p. 153) states in his elegy on Donne: 'The muses garden with pedantic weeds / O'rspread, was purg'd by thee; the lazy seeds / Of servile imitation thrown away; / And fresh invention planted'. Donne sought original ways of expressing the transcendence of love, demolishing the tired clichés of Petrarchan imitators. He introduced the ingenious 'metaphysical' conceit – a complex analogy that manipulates the similarity of apparently dissimilar things or emotional states in an unusual and often shocking way. Such conceits work well with the argumentative and analytical structure of much Metaphysical poetry, as the poet attempts to rethink poetry itself – on a philosophical level – in a changing world. This is not, however, to deny the fact that Donne, particularly when addressing female patrons such as the Countess of Bedford, made use of Petrarchan conventions.

Ben Jonson's classicism and the Cavalier lyric

The second poet with a profound influence on seventeenth-century verse was Ben Jonson. Jonson shared with Donne a need to produce a new poetic. But Jonson's poetic differs in his stress on proportion, harmony, moderation and decorum in language – an approach to literature which was heavily influenced by his love of the classics, particularly the work of the Roman poet Horace. Jonson maintained that poets were 'vatic' (prophetic) and, as such, must provide an ethical ideal for their society. In stressing the social importance of the poet, he raised the standing of poetry early in the seventeenth century. Indeed, Jonson (1996, p. 377) stated that there was a 'consociation of offices' shared by the monarch and the poet – that both were responsible for providing virtuous models of living. In his verse, Jonson held to his own ethical integrity and, increasingly, after his fall from court favour in Charles I's reign, to the group of young poets who idolized him. These he dubbed the 'Tribe of Ben', more familiarly and broadly known to us as the Cavalier poets, including Robert Herrick, Richard Lovelace, Sir John Suckling and Thomas Carew.

Though Jonson is known more for his occasional verse, his ethical views and stylistic influence are evident in the works of the Cavalier lyricists who celebrated the idealized relationship between Charles I and his queen, Henrietta Maria. These lyrics partake in the Platonism of the Caroline court, which is also evident in the masque and the visual arts. These conventions allowed Charles I and Henrietta Maria's virtuous, loving relationship to stand as an exemplary pattern for the ideal bond between a king and his subjects. Yet, within the court, there were voices that challenged the idealized conventions of Platonic love, particularly that of Sir John Suckling. Though a committed royalist – Suckling, as well as Carew and Lovelace, served in the Bishops' Wars – his work provides a sceptical interrogation of such conventions.

But there is more at stake than just literary conventions – whether, for example, as in Suckling's 'Upon My Lady Carlisle's Walking in Hampton Court Garden' (Maclean 1974, p. 262), a woman is a Platonic 'diety' or 'flesh and blood'. By the 1640s, Cavalier poetry rallied to defend Charles I's authority. The idealized representation of the king and queen clearly underlies the love lyrics of Robert Herrick (*Hesperides* 1648) and Richard Lovelace (*Lucasta* 1649). In such poems, the speaker's Platonic relationship with his mistress mirrors the speaker's relationship with his king – fashioned upon notions of devotion, loyalty and love which characterize an idealized form of political subjection. Indeed, in many such lyrics it is evident that true love can only exist within a Caroline Golden Age, a classical pastoral ideal where the monarch reigned as a benevolent sun ensuring a perpetual, fecund spring. Symbolically, the actions of Parliament are seen in terms of someone interfering in the happy marriage of the king and queen / monarch and subjects, as in Herrick's 'To the King and Queene, upon their unhappy distances' (Rudrum *et al.*, 2001a, p. 102): 'Woe, woe to them, who (by a ball of strife) / Do, and have parted here a Man and Wife: / CHARLES the best husband, while MARIA strives / To be, and is, the very best of Wives.' In addition, when the king and queen's loving relationship is marred by such insolent interference, the Cavalier's relationship with his mistress suffers. This enforced separation from, and potential loss of the mistress in the work of Herrick and Lovelace provides the poignancy underlying all Cavalier lyrics of the civil war and Interregnum periods.

The Restoration and the libertine lyric

The influence of both metaphysical and Cavalier verse continued through the remainder of the century, most notably in Henry Vaughan, Abraham Cowley and Edmund Waller. But in the moral climate of the Restoration, poets came to adopt a new attitude in the lyric. While the rakish attitude of a ladies' man is evident in many of Donne's profane lyrics, as well as in Suckling's critique of Caroline Platonic lyrics, libertine verse came into its own at the Restoration. Prompted by the royalist defeat and exile of the 1640s and 1650s, it was the libertine who attained heroic standing in the 1660s. This was accomplished by transposing the conventional martial tropes of love lyrics (i.e. the sword of the Cavalier) into the penis. The great majority of libertine verse is a purely hedonistic account of male conquest, often verging on the pornographic in the works of Charles Sackville, Earl of Dorset and Sir Charles Sedley. However, the Earl of Rochester's poetry is always critical of the libertine ideal. Rochester's more realistic, bloated, alcoholic, pox-ridden libertine speakers (the conventional attributes of the Cavalier stereotype in parliamentarian propaganda in the middle of the century) exquisitely point to the debased condition of the age, and most certainly reflect on Charles II's promiscuity and political indifference. Indeed, Rochester's critique of his world radically questions the limits of reason, faith and politics in 'The Fall' and 'A Satyr on Reason and Mankind'. He denies the penis the status of the phallus, symbolic of patriarchal authority (Clark 1995, p. 37). In Rochester's verse, the masculine libertine body fails and lays bare not only the sexual, but also the political impotence of Charles II (see, for example, Rochester's 'A Satyr on Charles II').

Rochester's deflation of libertine ideals is commensurate with the female libertinism of Aphra Behn's verse. In her 'The Disappointment', a pastoral seduction poem on impotence, Cloris reaches out to Lysander's penis only to find it flaccid. Again, the phallus – 'that fabulous Priapus, / That potent God, as poets feign' (Behn 1998, p. 226) – is a fallacy. These lines are a wonderful deconstruction of a less critical male libertine poetic, which may be characterized as Restoration priapic poetry. Much of Behn's verse exploits the political implications of pastoral. In this, she was not alone, as other female poets, such as Katherine Philips, recognized the possibilities of the genre. But, in Behn's case, she effectively uses the mode to interrogate ideology radically in such a way as to re-negotiate the gendering of political submission as it had been portrayed in Cavalier pastoral. Somewhat paradoxically in relation to its origin in a celebration of male conquest, Restoration libertinism allowed for a comprehensive examination of power relations from a female perspective.

Devotional verse

Donne's challenge to literary conventions in his profane lyrics is matched in his devotional verse. His *Holy Sonnets* (published 1633) portrays a very physical manifestation of the struggle of the believer to find union with God – a conflict influenced in part, perhaps, by Donne's own soul-searching which led him to convert from Catholicism to the Church of England (something of that dilemma is evident in his 'Satyre III'). What is so curious about Donne's sacred and profane lyrics, however, is that they employ such similar strategies of representation and argument. The speaker in a profane lyric reaches for a unique means of expression and argumentation, often for the purpose of seduction, and claims a transcendent significance for physical consumma-tion. In his devotional poetry, Donne's speakers also search for a means of expressing their inner turmoil. Whereas phys-ical love transcends its worldly context in the profane lyrics, the devotional lyrics are marked by the problem of often being unable to break fully away from the physical, prompt-ing shocking imagery, as in 'Sonnet XIV' (Rudrum *et al.* 2001a, p. 59): 'for I / Except you enthral me, never shall be free, / Nor ever chaste, except you ravish me'. While the profane lyrics may be meant to be a witty performance for a male readership, an element of sincere anxiety is clearly evident in the tone and imagery of the *Holy Sonnets* – one may be rhetorically clever with a mistress, but Donne's speaker in 'Sonnet IX' (Rudrum *et al.* 2001a, p. 58) knows that one cannot fool God: 'But who am I, that dare dispute with thee / O God?'.

The influence of Donne's devotional verse is most evident in the works of George Herbert and Richard Crashaw. While Herbert shied away from the physical, confrontational ele-ments of the *Holy Sonnets*, he worked towards bridging the gap between notions of profane and sacred love in *The Temple* (1633). Again, this involves a concerted questioning of the abilities of poetic conventions and language to represent desire; as the speaker of 'Jordan (I)' (Rudrum *et al.* 2001a, p. 133) poignantly asks, 'Who says that fictions only and false hair / Become a verse?'. The speaker of 'Jordan (I)' not only rejects the inspiration of the worldly beloved female as a motive for lyric, but also replaces the conventional fount of inspiration – the springs associated with the classical Muses – with the river in which Christ was baptized. In contrast to Donne, whom Jonson (1996, p. 462) once said 'for not keeping of accent, deserved hanging', Herbert is more attuned to the musical qualities of language. This is not necessarily a fault in Donne, as his versification effectively captures the processes of thought and inner turmoil, but Herbert is, in comparison, refined and his speakers are less egotistical. That humility allows the speaker of 'Denial' (Rudrum *et al.* 2001a, p. 135) to find God within and 'mend my rhyme'.

Crashaw, on the other hand, fully embraces the ritual and ceremony of the Laudian Church of England. Indeed, following Queen Henrietta Maria into exile, he would convert to Catholicism. Crashaw's conceits are more extreme than those of Herbert, at times surpassing the violence of Donne, particularly in his epigrams on church martyrs. But he is often discussed as the most decadent of the metaphysical poets for the bizarre extension of his conceits, such as his lines in 'The Weeper' (Rudrum *et al.* 2001a, p. 261) on Mary Magdalene's weeping eyes: 'two faithful fountains; / Two walking baths; two weeping motions; / Portable, & compendious oceans' (Crashaw 1974, p. 133). Even his position in the English literary canon is a rather uneasy one, as Crashaw is more clearly influenced by continental writers, especially by Baroque art and Counter-Reformation Catholicism. Crashaw's poetic, more so than that of other Metaphysical poets, relies on an extremely affective rhetoric which assaults the senses, perhaps even overpowering reason through sensual overload.

Metaphysical devotional verse continued in the latter half of the century, most notably in the work of Henry Vaughan and Thomas Traherne. But Jonson's poetic influence can also be traced in devotional verse. Though Jonson wrote few religious poems, his influence is evident in the classicism, proportion and decorum of the devotional poems in Herrick's collections, *Hesperides* and *Noble Numbers* (1648). Milton, too, whose masterpiece is the religious epic *Paradise Lost* (1667), betrays a classical influence in the religious verse of *Poems* (1645) – employing a number of genres and also translations of individual psalms. Translations of the psalms were popular with both male and female authors in the seventeenth century. There are also several notable female devotional poets, including Aemilia Lanyer and Anne Bradstreet.

Occasional verse

Occasional verse comprises a number of poetic genres: commendatory sonnets; odes; elegies (particularly prevalent compositions by both royalist and parliamentarian poets during the civil wars); verse epistles; and country-house poems. These poems marked events such as royal births, marriages and deaths; a visit to a country estate; and important anniversaries, persons or battles significant to the nation. Occasional verse was also written to negotiate a poet's social status, particularly in relation to patronage. Every major poet of the seventeenth century wrote occasional verse – Donne, Jonson, Milton, Marvell, Cowley, Behn and Dryden. Its social significance is evident in Dryden's appointment as England's first Poet Laureate in 1668. The creation of this office finally formalized the royal pension that previous poets, such as Jonson, had been granted by the monarch.

Many students are rather suspicious of such verse – panegyric, for example, often seems to be verging on sycophancy. But, at its best, there are subtle elements of criticism, or at least warning, in occasional verse. Jonson's famous country-house poem, 'To Penshurst', for example, ostensibly praises Sir Robert Sidney's estate and its owner's virtues. The poem effectively balances its consideration of Sidney's public duties with the leisure of the retired country life, and celebrates the estate as a divinely ordained social organism, a microcosm of the realm where both the lord of the estate and the peasantry know their social duties and obligations. Penshurst, like other estates, was an important bastion of regal authority in its locality. These ethical concerns are apparent in other country-house poems, such as Carew's 'To Saxham' and Herrick's 'The Hock-cart, or Harvest home'. But what is also interesting is Jonson's (1996, p. 97) assertion of the poet's cultural significance within this pastoral setting as he praises Sidney's benevolent hospitality to both king and poet: 'all is there; / As if thou, then, wert mine, or I reigned here: / There's nothing I can wish, for which I stay'. These lines link together Jonson, Sidney and James I in a patronage bond which is certainly meant to stress the hospitable welcome of the poet at other estates. Patronage concerns are evident in other country-house poems such as Aemilia Lanyer's 'Description of Cooke-ham' (quite likely the first English country-house poem) and Marvell's 'Upon Appleton House'.

Indeed, Marvell's occasional verse is particularly interest-ing for its profound consideration of both literary conven-tions and the precedent set by royalist writers in the genres he employs. Marvell (Rudrum *et al.* 2001a, p. 327) is particu-larly hesitant about the relationship between poetry and power, of a poet foisted into a politicized public sphere by 'climacteric' events. For example, in 'A Horatian Ode upon Cromwell's Return from Ireland', Marvell (Rudrum *et al.* 2001a, p. 58) contrasts a dignified Charles I on the scaffold, surrounded by armed men who 'clap their bloody hands', with a troubling closing statement on Cromwell's political ascendancy:

And for the last effect
Still keep thy sword erect:
Besides the force it has to fright
The spirits of the shady night,
The same arts that did gain
A power, must it maintain.

Although a less questioning note regarding the political events that have thrust the poet into the public sphere may be sounded in 'The First Anniversary of the Government under His Highness the Lord Protector' (Rudrum *et al.* 2001a, p. 356), one still must deal with the poet's ambivalent line that very self-consciously reflects on his social role: 'If these the times, then this [Cromwell] must be the man'. Are these, indeed, the times? That line from the 'First Anniversary' is a moment of profound significance in Marvell's attempt to come to grips with his 'times' as a writer.

But occasional verse is not simply secular in nature. The young Milton composed the religious ode 'On the Morning of Christ's Nativity' and contributed a pastoral elegy,

'Lycidas', to a Cambridge University volume commemorating the death of a fellow undergraduate, Edward King, in 1638. Again, this is not just a poem on King's loss – he and Milton may not have been that close, and the conventions of pastoral elegy mark the relationship as rather distant – but a poem critical of the Church of England and 'our corrupted clergy' (Milton 1991, p. 39). Whereas Milton used occasional verse in service of reformation, Crashaw wrote moving verse epistles persuading the Countess of Denbigh to convert to Roman Catholicism.

Epic

Epic was seen as the highest poetic genre. Milton announced his epic intentions in *The Reason of Church Government* (1642), a polemical prose work attacking episcopacy. But it was not until the collapse of the Protectorate and the restoration of Charles II that Milton at last accomplished that goal with *Paradise Lost* (1667). He followed this with a second epic, *Paradise Regained* (published together with *Samson Agonistes* in 1671). A brief comparison of Milton's successful epic endeavours with Cowley's failed attempts to compose an epic is instructive as an example of poetic genre and political engagement. Cowley (Rudrum *et al.* 2001b, p. 481), already a leading royalist poet in the 1640s, recognized that 'A warlike, various and a tragical age is best to *write of*, but worst to *write in*'. He abandoned both his first, religious epic, the *Davideis* (published 1656), as well as his second, *The Civil War*. Particularly in regards to the latter, events, as he states in the Preface to his *Poems* (1656), had conspired against *The Civil War* with the royalist defeat at the first Battle of Newbury on 20 September 1643. Cowley (Rudrum *et al.* 2001b, p. 481) abandoned his royalist epic when history transformed it into '*Laurels* for the *Conquered*'.

Milton's cause had also been lost by the time *Paradise Lost* was published, but the poem defiantly resists becoming '*Laurels* for the *Conquered*'. *Paradise Lost* is marked by a long period of composition – from sometime in the 1640s according to his nephew, Edward Phillips (1957, p. 1034). Satan, the figure which has most fascinated critics of *Paradise Lost*, may well reveal the development of the poem and its author's polemical engagement in political debates for more than two decades. On the one hand, Satan can be seen as a megalomaniac in attempting to usurp God's rightful monarchy in order to establish a tyranny. But on the other, it is interesting to note how, at times, Satan's rebellious pleas against the tyranny of God echo some of Milton's own arguments against monarchy in works such as *The Tenure of Kings and Magistrates* (1649) and the Latin defences. Apart from this rhetorical struggle – based on conflicting views of 'liberty' – Satan's character allows for a brilliant critique of martial heroism.

Epic is a genre which conventionally celebrates a national, martial hero, a fact that foiled Cowley's *Civil Wars*. In defeat, however, Milton's successful assertion of 'eternal providence' in *Paradise Lost* rewrites the genre by redefining heroism on a profoundly human level in Adam and Eve penitentially descending to the 'subjected plain' (Milton 1991, p. 618). But Milton accomplishes even more in *Paradise Lost*. The 'Good Old Cause' – the defence of liberty from Stuart tyranny in the 1640s, and the emergent republican arguments of the 1650s – is evident in the epic. It is there in Milton's choice of 'English heroic verse without rhyme', made to serve as an example 'of ancient liberty recovered to heroic poem from the troublesome and modern bondage of rhyming' (Milton 1991, p. 355). For Milton, the 'bondage of rhyming' is commensurate with the yoke of the restored monarchy: customs and traditions that fetter human potential. Though explicitly topical political statements are largely avoided in *Paradise Lost*, John Dryden clearly understood the political implications of Milton's poetic. John Aubrey (1957, p. 1023), writer of a large number of biographical sketches of his most significant contemporaries, recorded an interesting visit paid to Milton by Dryden:

> Jo. Dryden, Esq., Poet Laureate, who very much admires him, and went to him to have leave to put his Paradise Lost into a

drama in rhyme. Mr. Milton received him civilly, and told him he would give him leave to tag his verses.

Dryden's dramatic adaptation of *Paradise Lost*, the *State of Innocence* (published 1677), was never staged, but the text reasserts custom and tradition by 'tagging' Milton's blank verse (unrhymed lines of iambic pentameter) in order to make the work conform to Dryden's Tory politics.

Dryden clearly had his own aspirations of composing an epic. But, while history conspired against Cowley's attempt at a civil war epic, the Restoration did not resolve the Tory poet's epic dilemma: Charles II's reign also did not provide suitable material. Something of the problem is captured in Dryden's (1985, p. 109) prefatory epistle to *Annus Mirabilis* (1667):

> I have call'd my poem *historical*, not *epic*, though both the actions and actors are as much heroic as any poem can contain. But since the action is not properly one, nor that accomplish'd in the last successes, I have judg'd it too bold a title for a few stanzas which are little more in number than a single *Iliad* or the longest of the *Aeneids*.

Defeat, again, forestalled a martial epic celebrating the Stuart monarchy. Nor did Charles II demonstrate particularly heroic qualities. During the Dutch foray into the Thames estuary, when Admiral De Ruyters sank several English ships at anchor, Pepys informs us that Charles II was at his mistress' house chasing a moth.

Satire
As Pepys' comments on the king's behaviour suggest, Charles II was more appropriately a target for satire. The English failure against the Dutch led to the republication of Marvell's 'Character of Holland' (originally published in 1653) which served to contrast Cromwell's victories against the Dutch with Charles II's defeats in 1665 and 1672. Marvell would also satirize the king and his administration in 'The Last

Instructions to a Painter' (1667). Indeed, satire came to be the predominant genre of the Restoration period, along with the related mock-heroic (of which the Earl of Rochester's 'The Disabled Debauchee' (1675) and 'Signior Dildo' (1673), as well as Samuel Butler's *Hudibras* (1661) are fine examples). The significance of Restoration political satire reflects upon a long-standing trope in monarchical political discourse, the theory of the king's two bodies. This theory ascribed a body natural and a body politic to the monarch (a monarch's body natural is like that of any other human being, while the body politic is mystical and immutable):

> After 1660 this was palpably a damaged and questionable theory, for any notion of sovereignty which was founded upon the royal body had to take account of two scandals: firstly the execution of Charles I, the literal dismemberment of the king's body as a deliberated judicial and symbolic act; secondly the sexual exploits of Charles II, the involvement of the king's body in highly publicised promiscuity.
>
> (Hammond 1991, p. 13)

Dryden, however, struggles to maintain decorum in relation to the king, but in doing so, he points to the very problems Paul Hammond highlights above. Satire is a didactic genre, as Dryden's (1985, p. 204) brief definition in 'To the Reader' in *Absalom and Achitophel* (1681) states:

> The true end of satire is the amendment of vices by correction. And he who writes honestly is no more an enemy of the offender than the physician to the patient when he prescribes harsh remedies to an inveterate disease.

Although *Absalom and Achitophel* satirizes the Whigs – and particularly their leader, the Earl of Shaftesbury, a target again in 'The Medal: a Satire against Sedition' (1681–2) – it contains a prescription for Charles II. The poem uses typology to fashion the king as the Old Testament King David, a representational strategy that was prominent in poems celebrating Charles II's restoration in 1660. But, by 1681, the analogy is clearly strained when Dryden (1985, p. 205) writes:

> Then Israel's monarch, after Heaven's own heart,
> His vigorous warmth did variously impart
> To wives and slaves, and wide as his command
> Scatter'd his Maker's image through the land.

The image is patently ridiculous as a response to the king's promiscuity – though Dryden is trying to alert the king to his failings – but it is also meant to partake in an attempt to salvage something of the older theories of monarchy within the contexts of the Exclusion Crisis. However, Rochester's 'A Satyr on Charles II' (1968, p. 61) captures the king's promiscuity much more effectively and truthfully by focusing not on the king's body politic, but on his body natural: 'Restless he rolls about from whore to whore, / A merry monarch, scandalous and poor'.

We might, then, characterize the poetry of the period as an intense interrogation of traditional beliefs which had been severely shaken. The turmoil allowed poets to either lament the loss of a supposedly God-ordained hierarchy or seize on the opportunity to explore alternatives. Poets dynamically reworked not only traditional literary conventions and the politics inherent in generic forms, but also addressed their wider socio-political contexts, including language itself.

Drama

Jacobean transitions

Ben Jonson and William Shakespeare are figures of continuity with the Elizabethan stage. Through the first two decades of the Jacobean period, both men were at their creative height. While Shakespeare died in 1616, Jonson continued writing plays into the Caroline period, but these were not successful. After the failure of *The New Inn, or, The Light Heart* (1629), a comedy, Jonson (1996, p. 282) wrote his farewell ode to the 'loathèd stage'. Both Jonson's and Shakespeare's

Jacobean plays reveal the period's generic transformations and worldview – they engage with metropolitan life, the nature of political authority and intellectual doubt in a changing world. Through the Jacobean and Caroline periods, both comedy and tragedy shared a fixation for debased motivation centred upon what is now the standard fair of Hollywood movies: mercenary equations of sex, money and violence – though the Jacobeans and Carolines show a greater flair for originality.

The word one often encounters to describe Jacobean drama is 'decadence'. The charge can even be made against Shakespeare's 'problem plays' and romances – both of which demonstrate the developing taste for spectacle and artificiality which, at times, contribute to rather improbable plots. For example, Hermione's statue transformation in Act 5, Scene 3 as a means to resolve the plot in *The Winter's Tale* (1609–11): 'Strike all that look upon with marvel!' (Greenblatt *et al.* 1997, p. 2951). This may well work as entertainment, but in contrast to Shakespeare's tragedies of the Jacobean period, the emotional response evoked is rather hollow. Certainly, however, romance allowed Shakespeare to experiment with dramatic form, and he did produce important plays in this genre, most notably *Cymbeline, King of Britain* (1609–10) and *The Tempest* (1611).

Censorship

While the royal household patronized playwrights and players, it also influenced the theatre in one other important way – censorship. The office of the Master of Revels had been created by Henry VIII, ostensibly to manage the entertainments at court during the revels season between All Saints' Day and Lent. The Master of Revels hired the companies, paid them and approved which plays would be performed. By the early Stuart period, the Master of Revels' authority as a censor extended beyond just court entertainments. With the introduction of the anti-blasphemy statute in 1606, the 'Act to Restrain Abuses of Players', the Master of Revels' authority came to include censoring not only the performance of plays but also their publication, in conjunction with the ecclesiastical Court of High Commission. In other instances, royal displeasure and complaints from aristocrats or foreign dignitaries resulted in action against playwrights and acting companies. For example, Thomas Middleton's *A Game at Chess*, performed for several days at the Globe in 1624 during negotiations for a possible marriage between Prince Charles and the Spanish Infanta, prompted the closure of the theatre following complaints from the Spanish ambassador as to the anti-Spanish sentiment of the play.

Jonson's theatrical career best demonstrates the dangers faced by playwrights. Though he contributed to the aura of majesty by writing masques for the Jacobean and Caroline courts, Jonson found himself in trouble on several occasions. His first run-in with authority resulted in his imprisonment in Marshalsea in 1597 for the collaborative play, *The Isle of Dogs*. Jonson would be jailed again in 1605, along with his collaborators George Chapman and John Marston, for the anti-Scots' satire in *Eastward Ho!*: 'the report was, that they should have their ears cut and noses' (Jonson 1996, p. 468). The sentence was not carried out, but the *Eastward Ho!* incident had wider ramifications. The performance of the play, at Blackfriars, contributed to the Children of the Queen's Revels losing royal favour and changing its name to the Children of Blackfriars. Jonson's tragedy *Sejanus* (1603) twice landed him before the Privy Council for questioning – first, in 1605, 'accused both of popery and treason' (Jonson 1996, p. 469), and again in 1628 following the assassination of the Duke of Buckingham.

Jacobean and Caroline tragedy

Tragedies of state from 1603 to 1642 continued to follow the Aristotelean definition insofar as the plot centred upon the fall of a hero of high social standing – usually a general, king or aristocrat. In such plays, the fall of the tragic hero has not only a personal effect, but also points to wider socio-political malaise in society. The tragic hero's fall ends in his or her death while causing a significant convulsion that rocks the very foundations of the social order. Shakespeare's last great tragedies, for example, are wonderful accomplishments: *King Lear* (1604–5) strips away some of the majesty of a king, challenging the political notions which made a king analogous to a father, as well as exposing Lear, as a fallible man rather than an idealized king, to madness and the elements on the heath. The usurpation of the Scottish crown in *Macbeth* (1606) is also a brilliant achievement, which allows for a flattering portrayal of the mythic origins of the Stuarts.

The tragic portrayal of these high-born figures – be they mythical like Lear, historical like Macbeth or even fictional like Othello – exposed the political world on the public stage. Art in the period had a didactic purpose. Simply stated, art was to encourage virtue and denigrate vice. In terms of tragedy, the moral lesson is best summed up by Sir Philip Sidney in *The Defence of Poesy* (1595) (1983, p. 129): tragedy 'maketh kings fear to be tyrants'. Sidney's comment, in part, explains Milton's affinity for quoting the great Greek tragedians in his anti-monarchical writings of the 1640s and 1650s. Incidentally, the theatricality of kingship was often remarked upon by monarchs. For example, in *Basilicon Doron* (1599), James I (1996, p. 89) writes that a monarch must set a virtuous example for his subjects, 'for kings, being public persons by reason of their office and authority, are, as it were, set (as it was said of old) upon a public stage in the sight of all the people'. Critics such as Franco Moretti (2005) go as far as to argue that Jacobean and Caroline tragedy is a very direct engagement with wider socio-political trends which manifested themselves in the growing conflict between king and Parliament during the period and culminated in the execution of Charles I in 1649. In representing a king on stage, many of the theoretical underpinnings of monarchical authority could be called into question. In Shakespeare's *Lear*, for instance, the theatrical representation of a king may well betray that he is all too human. In addition, a play like Jonson's *Sejanus* (1603) lays bare the *realpolitik* of the court, and this may have contributed to the playwright's questioning by the Privy Council. Even the simple fact of an actor playing a king may suggest the potentially radical notion that the real monarch is no more than an actor playing a politically privileged social role.

Another form of tragedy became increasingly prevalent in the first part of the century: revenge tragedy. The inner struggles of Shakespeare's protagonist in *Hamlet, Prince of Denmark* (1600) reveal the psychological depth of revenge tragedy, which is present in the best work of the Jacobean and Caroline dramatists: Thomas Middleton's *The Revenger's Tragedy* (1606); John Webster's *The White Devil* (1612) and *The Duchess of Malfi* (1614); Middleton's *Women Beware Women* (1621); Middleton and William Rowley's *The Changeling* (1622); and John Ford's *'Tis Pity She's a Whore* (1633). Such plays demonstrate Sir Francis Bacon's (1995, p. 15) sentiments in his essay 'Of Revenge': 'Revenge is a kind of wild justice; which the more man's nature runs to, the more ought law to weed it out. For as for the first wrong, it doth but offend the law; but the revenge of that wrong putteth the law out of office'. The best revenge tragedies portray horribly corrupt societies that provide no legal or spiritual restitution to the wronged party, the revenger. It is often not the revenge which 'putteth the law out of office', but the corrupt individuals that represent social order, leaving the protagonist no alternative but to plot revenge. In the process, the personal revenge exacted by the hero becomes a social cleansing – a ritualistic blood-letting and self-sacrificial purge meant to reconstitute a harmonious, operative community.

Heroic drama

Heroic drama, the form of tragedy most prevalent on the Restoration stage, relied on spectacle for its effect much more than on the psychological perspective of the protagonist. In do doing, it loses the sense of social catastrophe which was such a strong element of tragedy written in the first decades of the seventeenth century. Set in an exotic locale, heroic drama depends upon its hero's emotional turmoil as he struggles between duty to his country and personal honour in order to attain his love, usually a woman who is the paragon of virtue. Beaumont and Fletcher's influence is strongly felt here, particularly through a play such as *A King and No King* (1611), where we find a similar, rapidly shifting emotional conflict which frequently lacks any particular motivation on the protagonist's part. The most notable author of heroic drama is John Dryden, and his finest examples are *Tyrannic Love* (1669), *The Conquest of Granada* (1670) and *Aureng-Zebe* (1675).

However, what is perhaps more interesting than heroic drama itself is George Villiers, 2nd Duke of Buckingham's brilliant parody of its conventions and artificiality, *The Rehearsal* (1671). Ostensibly a satirical representation of Dryden in the guise of the playwright Bayes, *The Rehearsal* (Harris 1953, p. 35) mocks the hero's sudden shifts of emotional state by equating a struggle he has with putting on his boots to his inner struggle as to whether love or honour is more important: 'Honour aloud commands, "Pluck both boots on"; / But softer Love does whisper, "Put on none"'. This speech carries on for 16 lines before Volcius hops off stage with one boot on and one off. Hence, even the protagonist's heroic standing is deflated, as Buckingham removes any sense of tragic empathy that an audience might have for the hero and essentially makes him a form of braggadocio – a boastful coward – in the tradition of Shakespeare's Falstaff. The epilogue of *The Rehearsal* (Harris 1953, p. 57) also calls attention to what was seen as the most blatantly artificial convention of heroic drama, rhyme:

> Let's have, at least, once in our lives, a time
> When we may hear some reason, not all rhyme:
> We have these ten years felt its influence;
> Pray let this prove a year of prose and sense.

Dryden defended rhyme in drama quite extensively in *An Essay of Dramatic Poesy* (1667). He argued that rhyme was 'natural': 'For the due choice of your words expresses your sense naturally, and the due placing them adapts the rhyme to it' (Dryden 1985, p. 93). For the interlocutors (participants in the dialogue form of Dyrden's *Essay*), rhyme is an issue of decorum meant to counter the 'liberty' of blank verse. However, in the Prologue to *Aureng-Zebe*, an heroic drama in rhyme, Dryden (1985, p. 183) acknowledged the charge of artificiality, as the poet 'Grows weary of his long-lov'd mistress, rhyme'.

By the time of *All for Love; or, the World Well Lost* (1678), an adaptation of Shakespeare's *Antony and Cleopatra* (1606–7) that is today considered Dryden's most successful play, he admitted defeat. In the complaint against critics in the play's Prologue, Dryden (Harris 1953, p. 254) states that the poet, 'gives himself for gone; y' have watch'd your time! / He fights this day unarm'd, without his rhyme'. The title-page of the play asserts that it is 'Written in Imitation of Shakespeare's Style'. In contrast to the earlier *Essay of Dramatic Poesy*, Dryden argues in the Preface to *All for Love* that Shakespeare's dramatic 'style', blank verse, is superior to that of French dramatists which had been seen as the preeminent model for playwrights immediately following the Restoration. Indeed, the Preface echoes Buckingham's criticism of rhyme in *The Rehearsal* when Dryden (1953, p. 247) states that the 'good breeding' of heroes in French literature 'seldom extends a word of sense'. Yet, while Dryden's *All For Love* is written in blank verse, like many of the Shakespearean adaptations for the Restoration stage, it bears little resemblance to the original play when reworked in such a way as to reflect late seventeenth-century dramatic conventions. What stands out most in this regard is Dryden's imposition of the three Aristotelean unities (time, place and action) upon Shakespeare's very episodic play.

Comedy

Whereas tragedy ideally dealt with the horrors of a socio-political convulsion brought about by the transgression of an exemplary character in order to reconstitute a harmonious community, comedy unified social order through laughter. Early in the century, Elizabethan romantic comedy – ending in social reconciliation through the marriage of its central couple – and comedies based on humoural psychology gave way to satirical comedies based on London life, the 'city comedy' of which Jonson's *Bartholomew Fair* (1614) and Middleton's *A Chaste Maid in Cheapside* (circa 1611–13) are fine examples. While the generation gap between parents and children, as well as the battle of the sexes element of courtship familiar from earlier comedy continue in city comedy, greed and sexual intrigue are the primary plot elements. In part, at least, one may suggest that economic forces which contributed to an emergent bourgeoisie led playwrights to focus on the ulterior motives for marriage in comedies at the expense of romantic attachment.

City comedy also satirizes other social habits, such as the popularity of romance literature. Francis Beaumont's *The Knight of the Burning Pestle* (1607) wonderfully satirizes romance by portraying an apprentice who decides to set off on an adventure in London:

> Why should not I, then, pursue this course, both for the credit of myself and our company? for amongst all the worthy books of achievements, I do not call to mind that I yet read of a grocer-errant: I will be that said knight.
>
> (Beaumont 1970, p. 17)

The satirical element of city comedy is also evident in its treatment of sexual intrigue. A couple of familiar subplots of this type of comedy centre upon greed and cuckoldry. In terms of greed, city comedy often explores the abuses of wardship (usually, a female who will inherit her father's estate and is under the guardianship of a rather unscrupulous individual who can arrange a marriage that is economically beneficial to himself). The cuckoldry subplot deals with the attempt to seduce a citizen's wife. While the conventional, romantic generic ending of marriage, symbolizing social harmony, continues in city comedy, it calls into question the economics and morality of the institution of marriage.

Cuckoldry and courtship would continue to provide the plot structure of the comedy of manners on the Restoration stage. A notable example of a cuckoldry plot is William Wycherley's *The Country Wife* (1675). In this play, Horner, the male protagonist, uses his wit and cynical awareness of social conventions in order to cuckold both citizens' and visiting country gentlemen's wives. He accomplishes this by spreading the rumour around town that he is impotent, and this allows him to allay the suspicion of the various husbands he cuckolds. The social conventions of courtship and marriage were also explored by playwrights in the comedy of manners. In contrast to the earlier comedic handling of courtship, the comedy of manners in the Restoration concerned itself – almost exclusively – with the developing relationship between two witty, upper-class lovers. Action was downplayed so as to focus on the verbal conflict between the male and female. The male, in particular, and sometimes the female, is a rake (the familiar libertine of much Restoration verse). Often, as a foil to the prime couple, plots depended upon a fop – a man of affectation and very little 'true' wit. His bumbling, however, shows off not only the artificiality of the social conventions portrayed, but also tends to highlight a disillusioned cynicism on the part of the main couple. For example, in Sir George Etherege's *The Man of Mode; or, Sir Fopling Flutter* (1676), the title character's affectation stands in marked contrast to the elegance and verbal sparring of Dorimant and Bellinda.

It is also important to note that our contemporary, academic English studies give us a rather skewed representation of Restoration taste and its relationship to the drama of the first half of the century. Neither Shakespeare nor Jonson were thought of as the most significant dramatist, but rather Francis Beaumont and John Fletcher. After Shakespeare's death, Beaumont and Fletcher became the principal playwrights for the King's Men, and by the 1630s had sealed their popularity which began with the success of *Philaster* (1610). The play sparked a vogue for a characteristic tragi-comedy that was widely imitated for decades. Beaumont and Fletcher's work reveals an indebtedness to Shakespeare's romances, on which they are reliant for spectacle, exotic locales and improbable plots. These dramatic elements are taken beyond Shakespeare's late-theatrical experiments and become rather histrionic. Beaumont and Fletcher's popularity continued, however, following the reopening of the theatres at the Restoration, as is evident in Pepys' *Diary* and Dryden's *An Essay on Dramatic Poesy* (1667). While Dryden (1985, p. 81) often expressed a respect for Shakespeare and Jonson, he found them, when judged against his neo-classical principles, to be rather uncouth in dramatic form, wit and language – and his contemporaries evidently agreed:

> I am apt to believe the English language in them [Beaumont and Fletcher] arriv'd to its highest perfection . . . Their plays are now the most pleasant and frequent entertainments of the stage, two of theirs being acted through the year for one of Shakespeare's or Jonson's.

History play
Whereas tragedy and comedy evolved early in the century, the history play slowly disappeared. While the Elizabethan and early-Jacobean tragedy often represented a historical figure (though we now recognize some of these as mythic, such as Lear), the history play as a genre gradually waned from Shakespeare and John Fletcher's *All is True* (also known as *Henry VIII*, 1613) to the last history play, John Ford's *Perkin Warbeck* (published 1633). The decline of this genre has prompted a critical thesis that asserts that the Elizabethan and early Jacobean theatres were 'national' in taste. The history play especially contributed to a collective, national vision and consciousness among the social mixing of all classes in the public theatres. But, as a result of the success of the private, indoor theatres such as Blackfriars, a more exclusive upper-class audience became the prime target for playwrights, in part, no doubt, because of larger profits. There was, however, a negative effect, as the more exclusive Blackfriars audience preferred a refined form of comedy and tragi-comedy. Hence, the more homogenous class make-up

of the audience beginning in Blackfriars imposed a particular path of development on the drama, the effects of which would be felt again at the Restoration.

Masque

Besides the public theatres, playwrights had another forum – the court. In addition to performances of plays first produced on the public stage, a particular dramatic form developed at court. Evolving from a combination of courtly entertainments, including music, dancing and pageants, and taking its place within the ritual theatricality of court life, the masque was a spectacular multi-media event. Originally, the masque centred upon the entrance of masked dancers, but it became a more elaborate form during James I's reign through the innovations of two men: Inigo Jones, who designed the sets and costumes, and Jonson. Jones is, incidentally, responsible for introducing the proscenium stage to England, and his ever more elaborate stage machinery and costumes contributed to the increasing expense of masques (and one must recall that, other than with rare exceptions, individual masques were only produced once). The masque proper was performed by aristocratic amateurs, occasionally even princes, princesses, and the king and queen. As a foil to the virtues represented by the aristocratic performers, Jonson first introduced the anti-masque in the *Masque of Queens* (1609). The anti-masque was performed by professional actors and added a symbolic, disruptive threat into the dramatic structure, though this was often treated comically. For example, in Jonson's (Lindley 1998, p. 117) *Pleasure Reconciled to Virtue* (1618), the anti-masque consists of Comus, '*the god of cheer or the belly*', and 'Pygmies', which, according to the Venetian ambassador's secretary, were dressed as frogs. In response to the presence of the aristocratic masquers and the monarch, the disorder of the anti-masque figures was dispelled, and all would come together in the final dance, symbolically unified and transformed by the benevolent presence of the monarch.

Masques, then, served an ideological function. The masque is for the king and queen. They are the primary audience around which the event turns – so much so, in fact, that the perspective vanishing-point of the set was the chair of state where the monarch sat. Hence, only the monarch had an unhindered view of the performance. Masques were also a means of displaying the aura of majesty to both the aristocracy and foreign dignitaries. But they were more than mere entertainment, as Jonson continually stressed. Increasingly, Jonson (1996, p. 346) felt that the ethical vision was being lost among the spectacle, which he once derogatorily referred to as mere 'painting and carpentry'. Jonson asserted that his words were the soul of the masque, while Jones' designs were merely the superficial body. The tension between Jonson's and Jones' vision of the masque eventually resulted in Jonson's loss of favour at court.

Though the masque is a highly symbolic dramatic form, the interaction of masque and anti-masque reveals an ideological structure which goes beyond mere sycophantic praise of the monarch's virtue – at times, the anti-masque may well present subtle elements critical of royal policy. Considering the moral laxity of the Jacobean court, this would appear to be the intent of Jonson's *Pleasure Reconciled to Virtue*. However, along with the change in moral climate at the court and the fashion for Platonic lyric, masques at the Caroline court presented the exemplary model of the loving regal couple, Charles I and Henrietta Maria. Carew's (Lindley 1998, p. 172) *Coelum Britannicum* (the 'British Heavens', 1634) presents them as the Hermaphroditic twin '*CARLOMARIA*' the 'Bright glorious Twins of Love and Majesty'. Through their virtues, they will transform the opening scene of dissolution and disharmony – represented by a city in ruins, Momus (god of ridicule) and the anti-masque of 'severall vices, expressing the deviation from Vertue' (Lindley 1998, p. 174) – to a glorious harmony.

The masque, then, defines a wider sphere of ethical action. Art itself does not dispel threats to virtue but, rather, provides exemplary notions for heroic action – a reformation of the soul that is 'impressing and lasting'. Jonson insisted on this. In his preface to *Barriers at a Marriage* (1606), for example,

Jonson (Lindley 1998, p. 10) argues, in a passage which is also relevant to his conflict with Jones:

> It is a noble and just advantage that the things subjected to understanding have of those which are objected to sense, that the one sort are but momentary and merely taking, the other impressing and lasting. Else the glory of all these solemnities had perished like a blaze and gone out in the beholders' eyes. So short lived are the bodies of all things in comparison to their souls.

The virtues incarnated by the aristocratic participants and the king and queen during the performance must emanate throughout the realm. Unfortunately, on the page, many of the intricacies of the masque are lost to us – and this not only in terms of understanding the elaborate choreography of its elements, but also of the significance of character, role, physical presence and interaction of aristocratic masquers and monarch during performance. William Davenant's *Salmacida Spolia* (1640) was the last masque performed prior to the civil wars, and the form was not reintroduced to the court upon the Restoration.

Drama during the Interregnum

Within two years of the last masque, and only months after Charles I's departure from London, Parliament ordered the public playhouses closed in September 1642. Recent critical work has examined Civil War and Interregnum theatricality and revises earlier views that claim the period was a void between the Renaissance and Restoration theatres. Susan Wiseman (1998, pp. 4–5) argues:

> The order which banned the theatre inevitably simultaneously foregrounded the role of theatre and drama as participating in constructing popular political debate . . . [T]he closure of the theatres served to intensify the politicised status of dramatic discourse. Civil War drama was sharply aware of its politicisation as a genre and of a political readership.

Both Wiseman (1998) and Smith (1994, p. 70) essentially agree that the closure of the theatres in 1642 'did not mean the extinction of drama, so much as a migration of dramatic resources to the arena of the pamphlet, and the partisan role which they played'. Plays continued to be produced in aristocratic households, in public venues and, occasionally, even in the theatres. Theatrical entertainments were also performed on state occasions during both the Commonwealth and Protectorate.

Plays continued to be published, and most interesting in this regard is the presence of short dramatic scripts (often in newsbooks) within the polemical contexts of the civil wars. Indeed, as dramatic resources entered into pamphlets and newsbooks, Parliamentarians continued to attack theatricality in relation to monarchy, while royalists argued for the importance of theatre. John Cleveland's *The Character of a London Diurnall* (1647) – an attack on parliamentarian newsbooks – provides an example of a royalist, satirical use of theatricality:

> The next Ingredient of a Diurnall is Plots, horrible plots; which with wonderfull Sagacity it hunts dry-foot, while they are yet in their Causes, before Materia prima can put on her smock. How many such fits of the Mother have troubled the Kingdome . . . and not yet delivered of so much, as a Cushion: But Actors must have their Properties; And, since the Stages were voted down, the only Play-house is at Westminster . . . Thus the Quixotes of this Age fight with the Wind-mills of their owne heads; quell Monsters of their owne creation, make plots, and then discover them, as who fitter to unkennel the Fox, then the Tarryer, that is a part of him.
>
> (Cleveland 1647, A2v–A2r)

But there is an element of wish-fulfilment in the royalist use of drama during this period: 'tragi-comedy provided the generic means for royalists to imagine the possibility of a happy ending for their plight' (Smith 1994, p. 77). This is evident, for instance, in the '*Joy* and *Dolor* . . . commixt' of the short pamphlet play, *Craftie Cromwell: or, Oliver ordering our New State. A Tragi-Comedie. Wherein is discovered the Trayterous undertakings and proceedings of the said NOL, and his Levelling Crew* (1648). *Craftie Cromwell* contrasts its satirical portrayal of Cromwell and his followers with a tragic representation of the king in order to imagine that possibility.

Prose

Character writing

Early in the century, two significant short prose genres emerged in England: character writing and the essay. Character writing developed from the classical Greek author Theophrastus' sketches, available in the early modern period in a Latin translation. These brief prose compositions portrayed defining characteristics of personality types. The first collection in English was Bishop Joseph Hall's *Characters of Virtues and Vices* (1608). Each concise sketch is, essentially, a stereotype of the subject's behaviour, manners and habits as representative of a trade, occupation, social class or gender. Throughout the century, for example, characters portray 'A Fair and Happy Milkmaid', 'An Unworthy Lawyer', 'A Wanton Woman', 'An Atheist or Most Bad Man' and 'A Romance Writer'. Characters are often juxtaposed in binary pairs, allowing for the explicit exposition of virtuous and reprehensible qualities. Such sketches are not solely limited to human stereotypes. Occasionally, an author may provide the 'character' of a geographical location and the people that frequent it, such as Paul's Walk. Located by St Paul's Cathedral, the Walk was the site of London's book trade as well as dubious night-time activities.

The most popular collection was the *Overburian Character* (1614). Though attributed to the Jacobean courtier Sir Thomas Overbury, the sketches it contains are by several hands, including the playwrights John Webster and Thomas Dekker. Their contributions suggest a link between character writing and the stock characters we meet with in the drama of the period. The *Overburian Character* was gradually expanded to over eighty characters in later editions (1615 and 1622), and its characters are much more bitingly satiric in intent than those of Hall and of later examples, such as Nicholas Breton's *The Good and the Bad, or Descriptions of the Worthies and Unworthies of the Age* (1616), John Earle's *Microcosmography* (1628) and Samuel Butler's *Characters* (circa 1668, published 1759).

Essay

While the character is basically a stereotype, the essay provided a more introspective exposition of an author's experience. Sir Francis Bacon published the first English collection, *Essays or Counsels: Civil and Moral* (1597). Modelled on the French author Michel de Montaigne's *Essays* (1580) – first translated into English by John Florio in 1603 – Bacon's collection contained ten concise prose pieces which were exceptionally aphoristic. The popularity of *Essays* prompted Bacon to issue enlarged editions in 1612 and 1625. In these, the original ten essays were revised and developed and new ones added. Bacon also achieved a more personal tone in the later editions, as he shared his opinions and experience on a wide range of topics: 'Of Truth'; 'Of Friendship'; 'Of Ambition'; 'Of Gardens'; and 'Of Faction', to cite but a few examples. As the full title of *Essays* implies, Bacon provides practical advice to his readership. His audience would appear to be men from a similar social background as the author who had to make their own way in the world. Bacon was a younger son, though politically well connected. In England, the patriarchal social practice of primogeniture passed property and status from father to eldest son, leaving the younger sons to pursue a career, often, as in Bacon's case, law.

As such, *Essays* is related to the genre of 'advice writing'. Most often, advice literature was written by a father to instruct his son on matters such as choosing a wife, preserving his estate, choosing servants and exercising temperance in wine. In addition to such worldly matters, advice literature also instructs its reader in moral precepts. Perhaps the grandest example of this type of writing is King James I's *Basilicon Doron* (1599). In the three sections of the book, James – from experience, backed by biblical and classical precepts – advises Prince Henry on a king's duties and obligations to both his subjects and God. Advice literature is not, however, limited to fathers instructing sons – many women also wrote advice for their daughters on domestic and moral issues during the seventeenth century.

Other notable essayists of the period include Owen Felltham, who first published *Resolves* in 1623; and Abraham Cowley, whose essays (published posthumously, 1668) are much more introspective than Bacon's. The essay, then as now, was also an adaptable form for the presentation of a variety of arguments. By mid-century, for example, female authors were writing essays that interrogated the premises upon which patriarchal society was structured, such as Margaret Cavendish, Duchess of Newcastle's *CCXI Sociable Letters* (1664) and the anonymous *An Essay to Revive the Ancient Education of Gentlewomen* (1673, attributed to Bathsua Makin). Such works challenge the status of women in society, arguing for a role in public life and for educational opportunities. In addition, the essay was effectively employed by Dryden to put forward his literary theories. Dryden's prefaces to his works are notable early examples of literary criticism.

Newsbooks and polemical pamphlets

The breakdown of the censorship apparatus in the early 1640s prompted an outpouring of published material, exacerbating the conflict between king and Parliament, Anglicans and Puritans and, later, Presbyterians and Independents. While the lapse of press censorship obviously had an effect on all forms of print, it is most markedly apparent in prose. One of the most significant prose forms to emerge in the 1640s was the newsbook. Newsbooks were not really 'books' but quarto publications – that is, eight pages in length. Prior to the early 1640s, there were occasional 'coranatos', newsletters covering events on the continent, as domestic news was heavily censored. Newsbooks appropriated all literary genres: prose, poetry and drama in their presentation of correspondence (much of it intercepted during the civil wars); Parliamentary Orders, speeches and debates; journalism; and religious and political polemic. Indeed, as Joad Raymond (1996, pp. 135–6) points out:

> The style of early newsbooks can be characterized as the absence of 'style'. The horizons of the newsbook were outwardly, not inwardly defined . . . It was the formal, typographical elements, the title and the daily heads, which defined the newsbook, while the text was essentially heterogeneous.

Early newsbooks were pro-parliamentarian. The first royalist newsbook was *Mercurius Aulicus* (published 1642–5), derisively alluded to as a 'court-libel' by Milton (1991, p. 253) in *Areopagitica*. The title translates as the 'Court Mercury', and many newsbooks of the period include *Mercurius* – the Latin form for the Greek Hermes, the god Zeus' messenger. Be they parliamentarian or royalist, newsbooks intended to draw converts to the cause by highlighting the political duplicity of their opponents.

Also prevalent following the breakdown in censorship was a burgeoning pamphlet debate consisting of controversial, polemical works on religion and politics. Certainly, these debates had begun much earlier, but censorship, particularly through the Court of Star Chamber, had meted out severe penalties which inhibited writers. The Presbyterian polemicist William Prynne, however, could not be stopped and twice experienced the wrath of Star Chamber, first for *Histriomastix* (1633) and then, in 1637, for several published attacks on the bishops and Archbishop Laud. For these latter pamphlets, he was pilloried, the remainder of his ears (cropped following the publication of *Histriomastix*) cut off, fined, imprisoned and branded on the cheeks with 'S. L.' – 'seditious libeller', or, as Prynne claimed, 'Stigmata Laudis'. But other more radical groups would also take the initiative to present their views to a growing reading public. With their political ascendance in the Commons, the Presbyterians came to realize the need for an effective means of press censorship in the face of religious sects such as the antinomian Ranters. Political groups, too, recognized the potential of print. John Lilburne, for example, eloquently presented the progressively democratic Leveller agenda, along with Richard Overton and William Walwyn. Lilburne, like Prynne, had been severely punished (in his case, flogged through the streets of London and pilloried) and imprisoned by the Court of Star Chamber in 1638. Other writers, such as Marchamont Nedham, newsbook and pamphlet author, began to put forth republican ideals through the 1650s. As Sharon Achinstein (1994) argues, the pamphlet debates which flourished during the 1640s and 1650s created a politicized public sphere as well as a vocabulary for political and religious dissent.

Women and polemical prose

Another fascinating aspect of the debate regarding political authority developed from attacks on the notion of paternal kingship. Milton's (1953–82, p. 327) statement in the *First Defence* is exemplary:

> We endure a father though he be harsh and strict, and we endure such a king too; but we do not endure even a father who is tyrannical. If a father kill his son he shall pay with his life: shall not then a king too be subject to this same most just of laws if he has destroyed the people who are his sons?

Such comments affected not only 'free-born English*men*', but also, of course, women. If we must not endure a tyrannical father, must women endure a tyrannical husband? There had been female authors who engaged with misogynist writers early in the century, most notably Rachel Speght in *A Muzzle for Melastomus, the Cynical Baiter of, and foul mouthed Barker against Eve's Sex* (1617). Female resistance would intensify with the civil wars and the Interregnum:

> The outbreak of civil war not only ended for ever the assumption that king's ruled by divine right and could not be challenged. It also released into print the voices of many women protesting against their confinement to roles of domesticity

and / or desired lady. The first great outpouring of published women's writing is concerned not with love and courtship, but with the structures of the public world and, crucially, with women's right to voice opinions on such matters.

(Hoby 1997, pp. 47–8)

Margaret Cavendish's work, for instance, consistently explores the 'structures of the public world'. In *The World's Olio* (1655), she insisted:

Thoughts are free, those can never be inslaved for we are not hindered from studying, since we are allowed so much idle time that we know not how to pass it away, but may as well read in our Closets, as Men in their Colleges; and Contemplation is as free to us as to Men to beget clear Speculation.

(Cavendish 2000, p. 140)

The figure of the closet (a small, private room) highlights the limitations placed on women of the period, and anticipates Virginia Woolf's 'A Room of One's Own'. Cavendish's *Olio*, *Orations* and *Sociable Letters* construct a female community from within this individual, private space and the contemplation it affords.

Devotional prose and religious polemic

Sermons were an immensely popular genre in the seventeenth century. Donne's *LXXX Sermons* (published 1640), as well as his *Devotions: Upon Emergent Occasions* (1624), demonstrate a flair for rhetorical and figurative expansion familiar in his poetry. The sermons of another Anglican divine, Lancelot Andrewes (first published in 1628), successively Bishop of Chichester, Ely and Winchester, as well as a translator of the King James authorized version of the Bible, avoid Donne's metaphysical rhetoric. But his style is interestingly characterized by an anecdote recorded by Aubrey (Rudrum *et al.* 2001b, p. 558):

He [Andrewes] had not that smooth way of oratory, as now. It was a shrewd and severe animadversion of a Scottish Lord, who, when King James asked him how he liked Bishop Andrewes' sermon, said that he was learned, but he did play with his text, as a Jack-an-apes does, who takes up a thing and tosses and plays with it, and then he takes up another, and plays a little with it. Here's a pretty thing, and there's a pretty thing.

As previously discussed, reason and science came to bear increasingly on theology, as did the ongoing debates on religion and political authority – apparent in the move from elaborate rhetoric toward a supposedly more practical, straightforward form of address. Evident in the works of Anglican clergy, the effects are felt most strongly in Puritan religious discourses, particularly as a manifestation of their grievances against set forms of worship.

The issue of 'smooth' prose style, then, is extremely significant as it manifests itself in religious discourse. While Anglicans were, and remained, reliant on 'set forms', Puritans claimed to be moved by the spirit and argued that 'set forms' both inhibited and falsified the devotee's utterance. For Puritans, their extempore pronouncements manifested the 'living' Word, which they contrasted with the 'dead' forms of royalist devotion. As Lois Potter (1989, p. 168) demonstrates, both Anglicans and Puritans:

> cultivated a 'spoken' rather than a written style and relied on an impression of spontaneity which was probably achieved in many cases by careful learning of a written text. Nevertheless, the dispute between those who defended 'set forms' and those who believed in improvisation was an explicitly stated one.

This dispute is most evident in pamphlets both attacking the hierarchy of the Church of England – by authors such as Milton, Prynne and the Independent John Godwin – and defending it, most notably those of Bishop Joseph Hall.

Another significant devotional genre was the spiritual autobiography. Individuals in opposition to the established church particularly favoured this genre which critically juxtaposed the believer's conscience against the worldly corruption of God's word. Notable examples are the Baptist John Bunyan's *Grace Abounding to the Chief of Sinners* (1666) and the Quaker George Fox's *Journal* (dictated in the 1670s). Both men wrote spiritual autobiographies while imprisoned following the Restoration, and their works point to both the motivations of those who felt 'moved' by the spirit and the persecutions they faced. Bunyan's *Pilgrim's Progress* (part one published in 1678), written during another period of imprisonment for his religious beliefs, is a more allegorical version of the spiritual journey than that recounted in *Grace Abounding*.

Religious discourses also provided women the opportunity to recount their own spiritual journeys as well as to admonish directly not only ecclesiastical abuses, but also political abuses. For many contemporaries, such works by women demonstrated another troubling aspect of the growth of religious sects. Some, such as the Quakers, allowed for a more egalitarian role that afforded women a voice within the spiritual community. Margaret Fell, converted to Quakerism by Fox, whom she later married, wrote to justify women speaking in church. Imprisoned on a couple of occasions for her religious beliefs, Fell continued to write pamphlets protesting the persecution of the Quakers. Female prophecy was also prominent during the period: Lady Eleanor Davies, for example, essentially a sect in herself, composed some 60 prophetic tracts addressed to the king, queen, Parliament and Oliver Cromwell between the accession of Charles I and her death in 1652.

Eikon Basilike

Perhaps the most noteworthy single publication of the civil war period for contemporaries was *Eikon Basilike* (1649). The book was purportedly written by Charles I, though the most likely author is John Gauden (the king's chaplain during his final imprisonment). The 'King's Book' is perhaps best read as a 'heteroglossic, collaborative royalist effort' (Daems and Nelson 2005, p. 21). It appeared on the streets of London, in limited quantities, on the very day of the king's execution,

30 January 1649. This was due to the indefatigable efforts of the printer Richard Royston. *Eikon Basilike* was immediately popular: there were 35 editions in England alone in 1649, with another 25 editions published on the continent (Madan 1950, p. 2). The book revisits the period immediately preceding Charles I's departure from London until his confinement in Carisbrooke Castle in 1647. Curiously, it is neither an expository narrative of events nor a political analysis from the king's perspective; nor is it a polemic. *Eikon Basilike* does not even identify explicitly who the zealous 'bad men' are who have persecuted their king and plunged the realm into civil war. The book, nonetheless, is an amazingly successful, affective text which justifies the preceding years in terms of the king's conscience rather than political apologia. As in the works of James I, *Eikon Basilike* seamlessly weaves together a text ripe with biblical allusions and scriptural fragments in order to portray Charles I as a king 'more sinned against than sinning' (Loewenstein 1990, p. 54).

Eikon Basilike also relates to the issue of prose style and the debate over set forms of worship in the Church of England. The book contains many allusions to the order and form of Anglican worship as opposed to the extempore 'zeal' of Puritan ministers. The claim to be spontaneously moved by the 'spirit' to extempore pronouncement that broke the conventions of established, set forms was seen by royalists as a troubling manifestation of the political rhetoric of 'liberty'. For the royalist, most notably, the issue is captured in a single phrase – Charles I (2005, p. 171) claims that set forms leave him 'better assured, what I may join My heart unto'. This statement points to an important link between *Eikon Basilike* and Cavalier lyrics. The king is, as the frontispiece of *Eikon Basilike* illustrates in its portrayal of a penitential king, the fixed rock assaulted by the waves of zealous, misguided men who have seduced the rabble to their perverse cause – the very forces which bring about the separation of the Cavalier and his mistress.

Eikon Basilike prompted both defences and attacks. The most important author to attempt to dismantle the kingly icon is Milton. In *Eikonoklastes* (1649, 2nd edition 1650), he handles the 'King's Book' in a fascinating way. While Milton recognizes the affective power of the book, he reads it as mere rhetorical artifice that has managed to gain a tyrannical hold on the imagination of its readers. Milton's goal is to smash that artifice in order to reveal the truth – a duplicitous king. He attempts to accomplish this by arguing that *Eikon Basilike* is a patchwork of literary genres. In other words, borrowed forms, many of them profane, that contradict the supposed sincerity of Charles I's devotional posture. Milton accuses Charles, for example, of 'sonneting' when he writes of the virtues of Henrietta Maria. In addition, he questions the sincerity of prayers based on the psalms, and discovers a plagiarized prayer from Sir Philip Sidney's *Arcadia* (1593). But most importantly, Milton argues that *Eikon Basilike* is overly reliant on the masque. In the Preface to *Eikonoklastes*, he identifies the title, emblematic frontispiece and closing Latin epithet of the book with courtly performance. Essentially, Milton (2005, p. 224) argues that the book is merely artifice:

And here may be well observed the loose and negligent curiosity of those who took upon them to adorn the setting out of this Book; for though the Picture set in Front would Martyr him and Saint him to befool the people, yet the Latin Motto in the end, which they understand not, leaves him, as it were, a politic contriver to bring about that interest by fair and plausible words, which the force of Arms denied him. But quaint Emblems and devices begged from the old Pageantry of some Twelfth-night's entertainment at *Whitehall*, will do but ill to make a Saint or Martyr.

While Milton may successfully call attention to the apparent disparity between Charles I's words and actions, his attack ultimately fails to dismantle the iconic king. Like others who attacked *Eikon Basilike*, such as the anonymous *Eikon Alethine* (1649), Milton could not break down the book's rhetoric of conscience. On another level, the failure may be attributed to the prevalence of literary notions of decorum, which Milton is oddly reticent to transgress. It is interesting to note that Milton is more successful in the Latin defences written in the 1650s, but in those works he is critiquing monarchy as an institution and demolishing authors supportive of the royalist cause – often by using *ad hominem* arguments (attacking the person, rather than his or her argument).

Prose romance

Romance reached a creative peak following the Restoration in the work of Cavendish and Behn. The genre had, however, been popular throughout the seventeenth century and, besides original works, there were many translations of continental romances. Originally adapted from Italian *novellieri*, prose romance, as Donald Beecher (1992, p. 32) notes, 'was a comprehensive medium, capable of containing nearly any aspect of contemporary social life. In practice, however, the emphasis fell upon love intrigues . . . presumably because audiences fancied the bizarre and titillating.' The comprehensiveness of the genre is evident in the most significant romances of our period. Bacon and Cavendish, for example, used romance to explore philosophical and scientific themes. Bacon's *New Atlantis* (published 1627) presents a utopian society founded and maintained on scientific and technological principles. As William Rawley's prefatory 'To the Reader' states:

> This *Fable* my *Lord* devised, to the end that Hee [Bacon] might exhibit therein, a *Modell* or *Description* of a *College*, instituted for the *Interpreting* of *Nature*, and the Producing of *Great* and *Marvellous Works* for the *Benefit* of *Men*.
>
> (Bacon 2000, p. 264)

Cavendish's *The Description of a New World, Called the Blazing World* (1666) engages with both the place of women in society as well as the scientific interpretation of a feminized nature. Indeed, it is possible to read *The Blazing World* as a response to Bacon's *New Atlantis*. Cavendish (2000, p. 153) writes in her Preface that the Blazing World is, 'but a World of my own

Creating, which I call the *Blazing World*: The first part whereof is *Romantical*, the second *Philosophical*, and the third merely *Fancy*, or (as I may call it) *Fantasticall*. The work is not a mere withdrawal into the fanciful, however, as *The Blazing World* revisits issues raised in her *Olio*, *Orations* and *Sociable Letters*, incorporating a critique of science, philosophy and political authority from a proto-feminist perspective – beyond the implied scientific chauvinism 'for the *Benefit* of *Men*'.

Romance was a genre that allowed female authors to engage critically with issues of gender and, particularly, patriarchal authority. Cavendish's *Blazing World* and many of Behn's romances accomplish this in an unsettling way. Romance often turns on the female protagonist's abduction and an implied threat of rape. The sexual violence is, however, forestalled, and the abduction functions to remove the hero from patriarchal strictures that inhibit female agency. Now alone, in an unfamiliar and often exotic setting, the female protagonist is allowed a limited degree of freedom to explore the world. In other cases, not abduction but some social or family catastrophe liberates the protagonist. This type of narrative frame is evident even in autobiographies of aristocratic women, such as *The Memoirs of Anne, Lady Halkett* (not published until 1875), as well as in Behn's forerunners of the epistolary novel, *Love Letters Between a Nobleman and His Sister* (1684) and *Love Letters by Mrs. A. Behn* (published posthumously, 1696).

The 'comprehensiveness' that Beecher identifies in the genre allowed for a fascinating exploration of contemporary events, as it does in Behn's *Oroonoko* (1688). Love is the motivating force of Behn's narrative, and she cleverly juxtaposes the slave trade, colonial exploitation and theories of monarchy with the love intrigue of Oroonoko and his beloved Imoinda. While *Oroonoko* is undeniably marked by negative racial assumptions, Behn (1998, p. 11) does link the fate of her protagonist to that of Charles I: Oroonoko 'had heard of the late Civil Wars in England and the deplorable death of our great monarch, and would discourse of it with all the sense, and abhorrence of the injustice imaginable'. Oroonoko's abhorrence of the execution of Charles I mediates both the narrator's and the readers' reaction to the execution of the protagonist at the end of the romance. Like Charles I, Oroonoko is barbarously murdered, a 'mangled king' (Behn 1998, p. 73), a royal martyr. As such, Behn's romance engages tragically with not only the past, but also with the political problems faced by both Charles II and James II.

MOVEMENTS AND LITERARY GROUPS

Metaphysical poets

There were no self-conscious 'schools' of writers in the seventeenth century. We can, however, trace certain affinities which have led to the three most significant groupings of the period – Metaphysicals, Cavaliers and neoclassicists. As noted above, Metaphysical verse is marked by elaborate, often erudite conceits: lovers to the legs of a compass in Donne's 'A Valediction: forbidding mourning', the spiritual struggle as a pulley in Herbert or the soul as a drop of dew in Marvell. Such analogies set the Metaphysicals apart from their predecessors and contemporaries by prompting us to reconsider the profundity of love or religious belief through the unfamiliarity of the conceit. More, too, is involved in defining the Metaphysicals than just their conceits. Their unconventional poetic metre, argumentative structure and diction successfully portray the psychological depth of their speakers' inner struggle in a fresh way in contrast to Petrarchan conventions which had become clichéd. In essence, thought and feeling dictate form, rather than poetic form dictating expression. Today we recognize Donne as the consummate Metaphysical writer, primarily for his verse, although his poetic is also apparent in his prose writing. Many of the characteristics of his poetic are evident in writers we identify as Metaphysical: Herbert, Crashaw, Marvell, Vaughan and Cowley. But Donne's influence is wider than just those now classified as the Metaphysical poets. For example, the Cavalier poet Thomas Carew occasionally relies on Metaphysical conceits, as does Dryden, the forerunner of the Augustans, in his early work.

We can see Donne's influence most strongly in devotional verse. He was friends with both Magdalen Herbert and her son, the poet, George Herbert. Herbert's *The Temple* (1633) clearly reveals Donne's influence, although Herbert avoids the more extreme rhetorical violence of Donne's devotional verse. Indeed, in point of diction in Metaphysical verse, Herbert's (cited in Martz 1962, p. 257) comment on 'familiar illustration' and the catechism of the Church of England in his *Country Parson* are significant:

> This is the skill, and doubtlesse the Holy Scripture intends thus much, when it condescends to the naming of a plough, a hatchet, a bushell, leaven, boyes piping and dancing; shewing that things of ordinary use are not only to serve in the way of drudgery, but to be washed, and cleansed, and serve for lights of Heavenly Truths.

Herbert's verse reveals the divinity in 'ordinary' things by cleansing them in such a way that 'Heavenly Truths' shine through their commonness. Crashaw explicitly signalled his debt to Herbert's *The Temple* by entitling a collection of verse, *Steps to the Temple* (1646).

Jonson and the Cavaliers

Jonson's influence is most strongly evident in the Cavaliers. The term includes a rather broad group of individual poets – from courtiers such as Suckling and Carew, who treated the writing of verse solely as a social accomplishment of their status; to the provincial clergyman, Herrick; and others who supported the royalist cause during the civil wars and Interregnum. Initially, there was a group of young poets, including Herrick, who idolized Jonson, these he dubbed the 'Tribe of Ben'. Jonson's 'An Epistle answering to One that Asked to be Sealed of the Tribe of Ben' demonstrates the key elements of what has come to be termed Cavalier verse.

These include friendship, hospitality, wine, a classical ethic in relationships' and loyalty to one's king:

> I wish all well, and pray high heaven conspire
> My prince's safety, and my king's desire,
> But if for honour, we must draw the sword,
> And force back that, which will not be restored,
> I have a body, yet, that spirit draws
> To live, or fall, a carcass in the cause.
>
> (Jonson 1996, p. 192)

Jonson's classical poetic and ethical views, along with the notion of loyalty to the king, are what most commonly define a Cavalier lyricist. These ideals combine in Jonson and the Cavaliers in what is often referred to as the 'Good Life', an integrated view of how one was to conduct one's life as a social being: 'In itself, Cavalier poetry reveals a consistent urge to define and explore the features of what constituted human happiness, and of which kind of man was good' (Miner 1974, p. 466). Unlike the Metaphysicals, there is a clear affinity of style and political allegiance to the monarchical social order in Cavalier writing. The poetic and ethical notions posit a 'golden mean', a restrained balance, in Jonson's work, between what he saw as the excess and indecorum of Donne and the social threat posed by the extempore rhetoric of Puritanism.

Classicism

Classical influences are felt in much of the writing of the seventeenth century – due, in large part, to the centrality of Roman writers in both the grammar school and university curriculum. Jonson's (1996, pp. 378–9) statement on the classics provides a useful starting point from which to consider their significance to authors in the seventeenth century:

> I know nothing can conduce more to letters, than to examine the writings of the ancients, and not to rest in their sole authority, or

take all upon trust from them . . . For to all the observations of the ancients, we have our own experience . . . It is true they opened the gates, and made the way, that went before us; but as guides, not commanders.

One was not simply to imitate slavishly the classical authors. Jonson's poetic ideal is provided by the Roman poet Horace. He translated 'Horace, of the Art of Poetry' (published 1640), and used Horace as the persona for his own view of drama in *Poetaster* (1601), in which Jonson satirizes his fellow playwrights, John Marston and Thomas Dekker. In contrast to Metaphysical writing, the classical notions Jonson developed, and were picked up by the Cavaliers, stressed decorum, an essentially conservative respect for tradition, wit ruled by judgement, and an understanding and adaptation of genre (both poetic and dramatic) through an engagement with one's world. Where Metaphysical verse is 'rough', the classical influence was tightly constructed and polished:

> The congruent, and harmonious fitting of parts in a sentence, hath almost the fastening, and force of knitting, and connection: as in stones well-squared, which will rise strong a great way without mortar.
>
> (Jonson 1996, p. 433)

But, while Jonson modelled his work on the writers of the Roman Empire, which was conducive to his political views of monarchy, other writers of the seventeenth century were influence by the literature of the Roman Republic. We can contrast Jonson's view of classical literature with that of Milton. Milton, closer to Puritan values, employed classical genres in his writing: for example, ode, epic and tragedy. Even his prose is marked by classical rhetorical structures. But Milton was uneasy with unquestionably accepting such 'paganism'. Indeed, a significant element of Milton's relationship to the classics is a process of Christianizing them rhetorically, generically and ethically. The most comprehensive example is the reconfiguration of epic heroism, away from the martial values debased in the representation of Satan, to the Christian couple, Adam and Eve, in *Paradise Lost.*

Neoclassicism

By the time of the Restoration, classical ideas in culture and literature would come to be influenced by continental views of Greek and Roman culture, particularly French tastes acquired by the exiled court of Charles II. Dryden is the exemplary author of this neoclassical trend, which is called Augustan, and finds its creative peak in the following century in the works of Alexander Pope and Jonathan Swift. Dryden's prefaces and critical essays judge literature through very strict rules. For example, though he does demonstrate a grudging respect for Shakespeare, Dryden finds fault in Shakespeare's neglect of the three dramatic unities – place, time and action – which were adapted by French dramatists from Aristotle's *Poetic*. Even on the level of 'wit', Dryden's English poetic and dramatic precursors were found wanting in the Restoration. Similar to the sentiments expressed by Sprat on the English language, Dryden, himself a member of the committee to improve the language, claims in *An Essay of Dramatic Poesy* that, 'our age is arriv'd to a perfection in it which they [Shakespeare, Jonson and Beaumont and Fletcher] never knew and which . . .' 'tis probable they never could have reach'd' (Dryden 1985, p. 97). Literary ideals, as in the work of Jonson and the Cavaliers, come to serve as an extension of a political worldview – in Dryden's case, Tory.

Neoclassicism, then, is another historically specific adaptation of a 'golden mean'. As in Jonson's work, Dryden strives toward a restrained balance of passion and reason; in part, this is most definitely a reaction against the excesses of Puritanism through the civil wars and Interregnum and bears the influence of the Royal Society's attitude to language. Restraint is most evident in the dominant verse form – not only in almost all poetic genres, but also through much of the period, heroic drama – of the Restoration, the heroic couplet (a pair of end-stopped, rhyming lines of iambic pentameter). The heroic couplet is particularly adept, in its precise balance, for the predominantly didactic function of Restoration literature. Taking advantage of that balance, the heroic couplet is a most effective verse form for satire, as it can extol ideas of order or, through antithesis, point to the faulty reasoning of a satirical target within its concise, two-line units.

3

Critical Approaches

HISTORICAL OVERVIEW

Critical views of literature are greatly affected by historical and social contexts. In Part 2 of this book, I have noted the contextual factors which played a part in how seventeenth-century writers read their literary precursors and contemporaries: Jonson's poetic and dramatic theories are presented in *Timber, Conversations* and his translation of 'Horace, of the Art of Poetry'; Milton continually reconfigures his own literary career in autobiographical digressions in his prose works; and Dryden's literary theories are developed in his prefaces, prologues and epilogues of his plays as well as in his essays. These authors developed both their art and critical views through a polemical engagement with their world, and this continues to influence our appraisal of their accomplishments. We are also, of course, influenced by the critical tradition of the intervening centuries.

The critical status of the Metaphysical poets is the most familiar example of how seventeenth-century critical perceptions of literature have established the parameters of later inquiry. Jonson's condemnation of Donne's versification, although he also made some positive comments on Donne's poetry, and Dryden's coining of Clevelandism ('wresting and torturing a word into another meaning') have already been cited in the poetry section. Dryden was responding to the excesses of Metaphysical poetry in relation to wider socio-political trends that had contributed to the breakdown of authority in mid-century, which he felt were recurring in the Restoration. The heroic couplet was the perfect form for him to express his ideals of order and balance. Dryden's Augustan successors perfected his restrained, conservative poetic as a bulwark of their ideas on the ideal, hierarchical social order. This continued to affect critical views of the Metaphysicals through the eighteenth and nineteenth centuries, as is evident in Samuel Johnson's familiar denunciation of Metaphysical verse in his *Life of Cowley* (from his *Lives of the Poets*, published 1779–81). Johnson's (1958, p. 470) reading of Cowley was harsh in asserting 'a kind of *discordia concors*'. In Johnson's (1958, p. 469) opinion:

> If the father of criticism [Aristotle] has rightly denominated poetry . . . *an imitative art*, these writers will without great wrong lose their right to the name of poets, for they cannot be said to have imitated anything: they neither copied nature nor life; neither painted the forms of matter nor represented the operations of the intellect.

His critical evaluation of Cowley became authoritative and marginalized Metaphysical poetry until the twentieth century. But the work of Donne and the Metaphysicals was positively re-evaluated by T. S. Eliot in 1921.

Undoubtedly, elevating Metaphysical verse to a privileged position in the literary canon served Eliot's own poetic goals in constructing a literary tradition. Contrary to Johnson's view that Metaphysical poetry was overly intellectual and merely clever, Eliot (1963, p. 112) suggests something far more comprehensive underlying their poetic:

The poet must become more and more comprehensive, more allusive, more indirect, in order to force, to dislocate if necessary, language into his meaning. Hence we get something which looks very much like the metaphysical conceit – we get, in fact, a method curiously similar to that of the 'metaphysical poets'.

This greatly enhanced readings of seventeenth-century verse, as well as our understanding of the English literary tradition, particularly in regards to the construction of the canon. Eliot's reappraisal down-played Jonson and the Cavaliers, as well as Milton and Dryden. Although Eliot slightly revised his opinion of Milton in a 1947 essay, he blamed both Milton and Dryden for a 'dissociation of sensibility' which, as these two came to be powerful influences on succeeding writers, had a bad effect on poetry. For Eliot, Shakespeare and Donne wrote a living language – an imaginative fusion of sensual and rational imagination. While he recognizes Dryden for maintaining a conversational language in his writings, Eliot felt that both he and Milton had given precedence to rhetoric. In part, however, Eliot's comments on Milton are coloured by his dislike of Milton's politics.

Eliot's writings on literature are related to the school collectively known as New Critics. New Criticism, through the 1920s to the 1960s in both Great Britain and North America, in large part, established English as an independent academic discipline. It asserted the primacy of the work of art in itself – as an autonomous artefact that uses language and constructs meaning in a particular way. New Criticism asserts a rigid distinction between literature and other discourses (i.e. the language of politics or science) and is, in many ways, indebted to the social conservatism of the Neoclassical movement. The work of the New Critics provided many key terms familiar to us as a means of critically approaching literature: imagery, diction, symbolism, etc. Approaching literary works through these categories, the New Critics claimed an objectivity in critical evaluation, an almost scientific means of appraisal that one brought to a text in order to ascertain its standing as literature.

Other forms of criticism – classical Freudian interpretations and historical and biographical criticism – during the late nineteenth and early twentieth century reflect the primacy of the work and the consciousness of the individual author. The objective stance is evident, for example, in E. M. W. Tillyard's *Elizabethan World Picture* (1943 (1972)). Tillyard provides the historical contexts (examining the imagery of a literary text against the structure of thought in the sixteenth and early seventeenth centuries) of Shakespeare's and Donne's work as mere 'background'. This allows the critic to read literature in such a way as to assert the transcendent genius of the author and the work – their ability to transform the common beliefs of their world into art.

However, the supposed objectivity and standards of evaluation of the New Critics gradually came to be challenged because of their underlying conservatism. In a curious way, the breakdown of New Critical authority is already signalled in Eliot's (1963, p. 113) essay on the Metaphysicals when he writes: 'Donne looked into a great deal more than the heart. One must look into the cerebral cortex, the nervous system, and the digestive tract.' Recent criticism has done just that – expanded its reading of literature to include contextual elements that New Criticism felt were insignificant to an understanding of the work as 'literature'. Indeed, the very distinction of 'text' and 'context' in some forms of criticism (notably, Cultural Materialism and New Historicism) has collapsed. Though not as tumultuous as the socio-political climate of the mid-seventeenth century, the 1960s spawned its own movements challenging traditional authority, and this had a significant effect on literary criticism. Beginning in the 1960s, schools of criticism emerged that would not only consider Donne's cerebral cortex, nervous system and digestive tract in relation to his writing, but also a whole range of issues that the New Critics had deliberately avoided. The New Critics may have helped to establish English as an independent academic discipline, but literary critics have been increasingly influenced by developments in other disciplines: anthropology and sociology; psychology; art history; gender studies; history; and cultural theory. This broadening awareness has undoubtedly served to enrich and enliven our understanding and appreciation of seventeenth-century literature.

CURRENT ISSUES AND DEBATES

Feminism

Feminist criticism was, arguably, the first wave of new radical approaches to the literary canon and the politics of literary criticism. Feminist critics began to ask a number of important questions regarding English studies by focusing on two issues: the exclusion of all but a few female authors from the canon and the representation of women in literature. Both of these tended to explode the notion of objectivity and the standards of evaluation put forward by the New Critics. With regard to the first issue, feminists pointed to the masculine biases that constructed the literary canon. One of the ways in which they did this was through social history: the fact that educational opportunities were denied women, and, therefore, the standards used to evaluate a writer favour male authors. The work of feminists has led to the inclusion of more seventeenth-century female authors in the canon, as well as genres which had been largely excluded. The most prominent text for undergraduate survey courses, *The Norton Anthology of English Literature* (currently in its eighth edition), is evidence of our enriched understanding of literature through the work of feminist critics. *The Norton Anthology* has, through successive editions, added more female authors and genres which had previously not been included. The broader critical repercussions of feminism include the reconsideration of the 'author' in seventeenth-century English literature, which had normatively been an educated white, Protestant male, and the unstable division of 'high' and 'low' genres which reflected the conservative elitism of New Critics.

We can briefly explore the effect of feminist criticism by looking at the critical construction of Shakespeare. In his preface to Shakespeare (1765), Johnson (1958, p. 241) claims that: 'In the writings of other poets a character is too often an individual; in those of *Shakespeare* it is commonly a species.' These views, like Johnson's criticisms of Cowley, continued to predominate into the twentieth century: for example, L. C. Knights' (1971, p. 233) statement that '*Lear* . . . is a universal allegory'. But, certainly, there are patriarchal biases in both Johnson's and Knights' comments which see the 'universal' human condition in Shakespeare's male tragic heroes. Feminist critics responded to these claims by returning to Shakespeare's text and examining why, for example, the male tragic hero's epiphany often involves the death of a central female character, such as, in Lear's case, Cordelia. Perhaps an even more disconcerting example of these critical biases occurs in readings of *Othello*. In his discussion of the play in *Shakespearean Tragedy* (1904), A. C. Bradley's (1971, p. 198) argument – and it is a recurring view in earlier Shakespeare criticism – reflects a questionable set of assumptions regarding the murder of Desdemona and its aftermath:

> And pity itself vanishes, and love and admiration alone remain, in the majestic dignity and sovereign ascendancy of the close. Chaos has come and gone . . . [leaving] a greater and nobler Othello . . . and when he dies upon a kiss the most painful of all tragedies leaves us for the moment free from pain, and exulting in the power of 'love and man's unconquerable mind'.

But, obviously, Desdemona, who Bradley (1971, p. 201) sees as 'the "eternal womanly" in its most lovely and adorable form', is murdered in order for Othello to arrive at this noble, transcendent 'truth'. Feminist critics of Shakespeare quite rightly turned the transcendent bard into a cultural battleground, and this has expanded to include all authors of the seventeenth century. Today, as a result, we are much more sensitive readers of the sexual politics of representation in the early modern period, of how female characters are constructed through literary conventions.

Feminist criticism has also wonderfully addressed wider political issues; for example, Catherine Gallagher's (1988) insightful discussion of the paradox of Tory proto-feminism in the works of Behn and the Duchess of Newcastle. Gallagher reads the seventeenth-century socio-political status of women against political discourses which deprived them of rights. In doing so, she argues that female authors espousing Tory views (rather than those influenced by the Whig ideal of individuality and limits on monarchical authority or the egalitarian ideals of some of the religious sects) negotiated and posited increasing freedom against the most powerful male figure of their society – the king. This sort of analysis is important also within the political debates on authority that developed through the middle of the century, particularly the issue of the social contract in Hobbes' work. Victoria Kahn (1997), too, has done important work on the issue of consent in relation to theories of political or social contract in respect to women in the seventeenth century. Her research examines patriarchal kingship and the politicized marriage analogy (the king as husband of the realm):

> one could say that the point of the analogy was to naturalize and romanticize absolute sovereignty by making it seem that the subject, like the wife, was both naturally inferior and had consented to such inferior status out of affection. Yet while such a contract was originally predicated upon consent of the governed (or the wife), once it had been agreed to, the contract was irrevocable.
>
> (Kahn 1997, pp. 531–2)

These approaches have been developed in readings of prose romance because of the centrality of sexual intrigue in that genre, but they are certainly relevant in the study of other prose genres, drama and poetry of the period.

Gender studies and queer theory

Following from feminism, gender studies has expanded to explore the way in which literature contributed to the construction and reinforcement of masculinity. As critics such as Andrew Williams (1999), Mark Breitenberg (1996) and Laura Levine (1994) have shown, masculinity in the seventeenth century was seen as radically unstable, and males needed to exercise constant diligence in order to maintain it. While male superiority was generally accepted in the seventeenth century, and females were seen as potentially chaotic threats to the social order if not kept in their place, the anxieties prompted by masculinity clearly undercut the self-assuredness of such an assumption. For Breitenberg and Levine, such anxieties are most apparent in the prevalent use of cuckoldry plots and the anti-theatrical attack on boy actors playing female roles.

Gender studies has also led to the critical inquiries of queer theory. Whereas feminist criticism explores the marginalization of women in literature and society, queer theory examines the same in relation to gays and lesbians. Both critical schools grew out of twentieth-century social movements in the 1960s, but, in the case of queer readings of sixteenth- and seventeenth-century literature, the impetus came from the notorious U. S. Supreme Court decision in *Bowers v. Hardwick* (1986). While the court found the buggery statute of Henry VIII, reaffirmed in succeeding reigns, as the legal precedent for Georgia's sodomy laws – essentially arguing that 'sodomy is always and everywhere the same, always and everywhere opprobriated, always and everywhere joined in a purportedly stable equation with homosexual identity' (Halley 1994, p. 15) – the sixteenth- and seventeenth-century understanding of the term can not simply be elided with our contemporary notion of homosexuality. Doing so is anachronistic, as 'homosexual' is a term developed in the nineteenth century. This has prompted Jonathan Goldberg (1992) to make the radical claim that, in the Renaissance, there were no homosexuals.

If we look at literature, along with other discourses of the period, we realize that gender and sexual categories were quite different from our own. We also find the term 'sodomy' itself extremely problematic. For example, in *Basilicon Doron*, James I (1996, p. 117) instructed Prince Henry that there are 'some horrible crimes that ye are bound in conscience never to forgive, such as witchcraft, willful murder, incest (especially within the degrees of consanguinity), sodomy, poisoning, and false coin'. As Alan Bray's (1995) and John Boswell's (1980) historical research has shown, 'sodomy' charges were most often secondary to some other 'horrible crime' of the sort James I mentions. In fact, James I's relationship with George Villiers, Duke of Buckingham did not, apparently, prompt James to consider himself a 'sodomite'. Bray's and Boswell's research has been developed by literary critics in relation to a prevalent homoeroticism in works of the seventeenth century: the boy actor on the pre-Civil War stage, and even genre, especially pastoral. But queer theory is not limited to male same-sex desire. Though male same-sex relationships were clearly seen, at least at the discursive level of the word 'sodomy', as a greater threat to social order in the seventeenth century, female same-sex desire has also been explored in the work of Valerie Traub (1992) and Lillian Faderman (1981).

Cultural materialism and new historicism

Other critical theories attuned to the 'cultures of subordinate and marginalized groups' also emerged in the latter half of the twentieth century. Jonathan Dollimore and Alan Sinfield's *Political Shakespeare* (1994) is a groundbreaking example of Cultural Materialism, which developed from the work of Raymond Williams and other British cultural theorists. As Dollimore and Sinfield (1994, p. 4) state:

> Materialist criticism refuses to privilege 'literature' in the way that literary criticism has done hitherto; as Raymond Williams argued in an important essay, 'we cannot separate literature and

art from other kinds of social practice, in such a way as to make them subject to quite special and distinct laws'. This approach necessitates a radical contextualising of literature which eliminates the old divisions between literature and its 'background', text and context.

Note, in the above quotation, the explicit challenge to the idealism of the New Critics and the divisions that their critical practice constructed between 'literature' and background, as well as the autonomous, privileged 'laws' of a literary work as opposed to other forms of social practice. Cultural Materialism is a form of Marxist literary criticism; but, while earlier Marxist readings of seventeenth-century literature had been somewhat limited in relation to their classical, economic Marxism, Cultural Materialism broadens its focus. It is indebted to the semiotic approach of structuralism and post-structuralism, which examines the rules and conventions of sign systems (not only language as a sign system, but also the rules and conventions of visual representation and how meaning is constructed within a culture).

Hence, Cultural Materialists may read an agriculture handbook of the seventeenth century alongside a pastoral poem, or an aristocratic family portrait by Sir Anthony Van Dyck alongside a masque. These different modes of conveying meaning within a culture point to the fact that, when political issues are added to the reading, all forms of cultural intercourse share representational strategies in order to produce meaning. Like its North American version, New Historicism (which, however, tends to efface its intellectual origins in Marxism), Cultural Materialism reads early modern literature as an intervention in and negotiation of its socio-political contexts, as literature is one of the ways that men and women transmit, explore and reinforce 'culture'.

Post-colonial theory

Post-colonial criticism examines the marginalisation of the racial 'other'. This form of criticism also developed in response to socio-political events in the twentieth century: the breakdown of imperialism, especially the British Empire. By the end of the period covered in this book, England was moving toward the establishment of empire through its trade activities. Early forms of criticism which maintained a distinction between 'literature' and 'background' did not explicitly interrogate the representation of either race or ethnicity in early modern literature. Much like the questions feminists began to ask in reading both literature and criticism, postcolonial critics examine how the representation of race and ethnicity in literary works play a part in producing the meaning of the text. They will draw upon travel narratives and accounts of overseas voyages in order to contextualize common racial and ethnic stereotypes of African peoples ('Moors'), American aboriginals and, somewhat closer to England, the Catholic Irish. For example, we meet with many 'Moors' in seventeenth-century literature, most notably Behn's *Oroonoko* and Shakespeare's *Othello*. What does Othello's tragedy tell us about early modern notions of the racial 'other'? Does the play uphold seventeenth-century perceptions of 'Moors' or challenge the supposed superiority of European Christianity as a civilizing force against barbarism?

The curiosity of seventeenth-century writers for other races and cultures was also spurred by the 'discovery' of the Americas. The conflict developing in the 'New World' between the aspirations of Spain and those of England provide a particularly fruitful set of resources to examine the representation of 'other' cultures. England generally attempted to portray itself as a kinder, civilizing colonizer in contrast to the demonized, gold-hungry Spaniards. The meeting of three cultures – aboriginal, English and Spanish – alerts us to the instability of the binary opposition that colonialism is dependent upon: civilized/barbaric. The rhetorical use of this binary is fascinating in both early modern colonial writings as well as allusions to the Americas in literary works. For example, up until the Jamestown massacre in 1622, the full brunt of the 'barbaric' opposition was put upon the Spaniards, while portraying the aboriginal peoples as innocents in a state of nature (see Evans 1996). As the work of post-colonial critics demonstrates, the European encounter with other peoples and cultures prompted many seventeenth-century writers to question their own culture and identity in an attempt, often, to maintain the civilized/barbaric binary.

Resources for Independent Study

CHRONOLOGY OF KEY HISTORICAL AND CULTURAL EVENTS

1603 Elizabeth I dies, accession of James I; 'Millenary Petition'; Jonson's *Sejanus* (tragedy); Florio's translation of Montaigne; Shakespeare's *Measure for Measure* and *Othello*; Shakespeare's company becomes the King's Men

1604 Hampton Court Conference; first session of James' first parliament; Treaty of London ends conflict with Spain; Marston's *The Malcontent* (tragedy); circa 1604–6 Middleton's *A Trick to Catch the Old One* (comedy)

1605 The Gunpowder Plot; Bacon's *Advancement of Learning*; Sir Thomas Browne, author and doctor, born; Shakespeare's *King Lear*; Marston, Chapman, and Jonson imprisoned for the collaborative play, *Eastward Ho!* (satire)

1606 Shakespeare's *Macbeth*; Jonson's *Volpone* (comedy); Middleton's (or Cyril Tourneur's) *Revenger's Tragedy*

1607 Flight of Tyrone and other Irish Earls, leading to land confiscations and plantation of Ulster; founding of colony at Jamestown, Virginia; Fletcher and Beaumont's *Knight of the Burning Pestle* (comedy)

1608 John Milton born; Shakespeare's *Coriolanus*

1609 Birth of Edward Hyde, later Earl of Clarendon; birth of Sir John Suckling; publication of Shakespeare's *Sonnets* (written earlier); Shakespeare's *Cymbeline*; Kepler's *New Astronomy*; Samuel Cooper, painter, born

1610 Fourth and fifth sessions of James' first parliament; Jonson's *Alchemist* (comedy)

1611 Publication of Authorized Version of the Bible (King James Bible); Shakespeare's *The Tempest*; circa 1611 Middleton and Dekker's *The Roaring Girl or Moll Cutpurse* (comedy); Beaumont and Fletcher's *A King and No King* (tragi-comedy); Aemilia Lanyer's *Salve Deus Rex Judaeorum*

1612 Contract made for marriage of Princess Elizabeth and Elector Palatine; death of Prince Henry; second edition of Bacon's *Essays*; Anne Bradstreet, poet, born; Samuel Butler, poet, born; publication of Webster's *The White Devil* (revenge tragedy)

1613 Marriage of James I and Queen Anne's only daughter, Elizabeth, and the Elector Palatine; Bacon appointed Attorney-General; Richard Crashaw born; Elizabeth Cary's *The Tragedy of Mariam* published

1614 The Addled Parliament; Sir Walter Ralegh's *History of the World*; John Webster's *Duchess of Malfi* (revenge tragedy); 1614–16, George Chapman's translation of *The Odyssey*; Jonson's *Bartholomew Fair* (comedy)

1615 James I proceeds with Spanish marriage negotiations, which provide for a Catholic succession; Inigo Jones becomes Surveyor of the King's Works; John Lilburne, Leveller leader, born

1616 Ralegh released from Tower and prepares for voyage to Guiana; Bacon becomes a privy councillor; Shakespeare dies; publication of James I's *Works*; publication of Jonson's *Works*; Jonson awarded a royal pension

1617 Bacon appointed Lord Keeper of the Great Seal; Ralegh leaves on Guiana voyage

1618 Bacon becomes Lord Chancellor; Ralegh executed; Bohemian revolt against Habsburg rule begins Thirty Years War on the continent; Abraham Cowley born; Richard Lovelace born; Sir Peter Lely, painter, born; Jonson's *Pleasure Reconciled to Virtue* (masque)

1619 Buckingham made Lord High Admiral; death of Queen Anne; James I voices approval of Synod of Dort's denunciation of Arminian beliefs; Frederick, Elector Palatine chosen King of Bohemia; Inigo Jones begins work on banqueting house at Whitehall; Harvey outlines 'discovery' of the circulation of blood at lectures at St Bartholomew's Hospital, London

1620 Battle of White Mountain, Frederick, Elector Palatine, loses Bohemia; secret treaty between England and Spain for the marriage of Charles, Prince of Wales, and the Spanish Infanta; Bacon's *Novum Organum*; Lucy Hutchinson, author, born

1621 James I's third parliament meets; impeachment and fall of Bacon; Burton's *Anatomy of Melancholy*; Massinger's *A New Way to Pay Old Debts*; 1621/2 Henry Vaughan, poet, born; circa 1621 Middleton's *Women Beware Women* (tragedy); Andrew Marvell born; Anthony Ashley Cooper (later Earl of Shaftesbury), leader of the Whigs, born; Lady Mary Wroth's prose romance, *The Countess of Montgomery's Urania* (with the sonnet sequence *Pamphilia to Amphilanthus*)

1622 Donne's sermons published; George Sandys' translation of Ovid's *Metamorphoses*; Middleton and Rowley's *The Changeling*

1623 Charles and Buckingham's incognito voyage to Spain; Margaret Cavendish, author and future Duchess of Newcastle, born

1624 James' fourth parliament; French marriage treaty for Prince Charles and Henrietta Maria

1625 Death of James I, accession of Charles I; marriage of Charles I and Henrietta Maria; Charles' first parliament; Daniel Mytens appointed painter to Charles I; war with Spain; final edition of Bacon's *Essays*; death of Webster

1626 Charles' second parliament, which attempts to impeach Buckingham; Bacon dies; Robert Boyle, scientist and member of the Royal Society, born

1627 William Laud appointed to Privy Council; war with France; posthumous publication of Bacon's *New Atlantis*; death of Middleton

1628 First session of Charles' third parliament; Petition of Right; assassination of Buckingham; Laud appointed bishop of London; John Bunyan born; Harvey's 'discovery' published

1629 Second session of Charles' third parliament, Charles dissolves parliament (beginning of 'personal rule'); Thomas Wentworth appointed to the Privy Council; Rubens in England on a diplomatic mission from Philip IV of Spain, does some work for Charles I and is knighted by the king; Jonson's *The New Inn* (comedy) fails

1630 Birth of Prince Charles (future Charles II); Treaty of Madrid ends Spanish conflict; Thomas Carew, poet, appointed Sewer in Ordinary to the King

1631 Death of Donne; John Dryden born

1632 Thomas Wentworth, later Earl of Strafford, appointed Lord Deputy of Ireland; Van Dyck becomes court painter to the king; William Harvey appointed king's physician; second folio edition of Shakespeare; John Locke born; Sir Christopher Wren born; Aurelian Townshend's *Tempe Restored* (masque); Katherine Philips, poet, born

1633 Charles I's Scottish coronation; Laud appointed Archbishop of Canterbury; birth of Prince James (future James II); Herbert's *The Temple*; first publication of Donne's *Poems*; Samuel Pepys born; William Prynne's antitheatrical tract, *Histriomastix*; publication of Ford's plays, including *'Tis Pity She's a Whore* (revenge tragedy) and the last history play of the period, *Perkin Warbeck*

1634   Star Chamber sentence costs Prynne his ears; first writ of Ship Money; Carew's *Coelum Britannicum* (masque); Milton's *Masque Presented at Ludlow Castle* (*Comus*)

1635   Second writ of Ship Money, extended to include inland counties; Robert Hooke, scientist and member of the Royal Society, born

1636   William Juxon, Bishop of London, appointed Lord Treasurer; third writ of Ship Money

1637   Burton, Bastwick, and Prynne mutilated for pamphlets attacking Arminian bishops; Hampden's Case; John Lilburne before Star Chamber; Papal envoy received at Court; New Prayer Book imposed on Scotland; Jonson dies

1638   Scottish National Covenant; Lilburne before court of Star Chamber, flogged through the streets and pilloried; Milton's 'Lycidas;' Suckling's *Aglaura* performed at court

1639   First Bishops' War, ends with the Pacification of Berwick; Wentworth returns from Ireland; Elizabeth Cary dies, buried in Henrietta Maria's private chapel

1640   Wentworth created Earl of Strafford and Lord Lieutenant of Ireland; Short Parliament; Second Bishops' War, ends with Treaty of Ripon; the Long Parliament convenes; 'Root and Branch' petition; press censorship breaks down; second posthumous edition of Jonson's *Works*, including *Timber*; Walton's *Life of Donne*; death of Thomas Carew (*Poems* published 1640/1); Donne's *LXXX Sermons* published; William Wycherley, playwright, born; William Davenant's *Salmacida Spolia* (last Caroline masque)

1641   Triennial Act; act against dissolving Parliament without its own consent; execution of Strafford; prerogative courts abolished; Irish Rebellion begins; Grand Remonstrance; Aphra Behn born; Suckling implicated in Army Plot, flees to France and, presumably, dies there

1642   Attempt to arrest the Five Members; the King leaves London; Militia Ordinance passed; Charles raises his standard at Nottingham; Battle of Edgehill; closure of theatres by Parliament; Sir Isaac Newton born; Lovelace presents Kentish Petition to Parliament, for which he is imprisoned for two months; two unauthorized editions of Thomas Browne's *Religio Medici* published

1643 Parliament establishes the Westminster Assembly to create a religious settlement; Solemn League and Covenant between Parliament and the Scots; John Pym, influential parliamentary opponent of the king, dies; Parliament revives censorship; Gilbert Burnet, biographer of John Wilmot, 2nd Earl of Rochester and a bishop, born; Margaret Lucas (Cavendish) joins Henrietta Maria's court at Oxford as a maid of honour; Milton's *Doctrine and Discipline of Divorce*; first authorized edition of Browne's *Religio Medici*

1644 Scots' army crosses into England; Battle of Marston Moor; Directory of Worship approved by Westminster Assembly; Milton's *Areopagitica*; Henrietta Maria and her court leave for France

1645 Laud executed; Directory of Worship approved by Parliament; Prayer Book prohibited; Uxbridge negotiations between the king and Parliament fail; creation of New Model Army, Fairfax as commander-in-chief; Battle of Naseby; compositions with royalists begin; founding of Philosophical Society (origin of the later Royal Society)

1646 Establishment of Presbyterian Church system by Parliament; Charles I surrenders to the Scots; Newcastle Propositions presented by Parliament to the king; offices of bishop and archbishop abolished; Vaughn's *Poems*; *Poems of Mr. John Milton* published (dated 1645); 1646–56 Abraham Cowley, poet, in exile with, and employed by Queen Henrietta Maria in France; Crashaw's *Steps to the Temple* and *Delights of the Muses*; Margaret Lucas marries William Cavendish, Duke of Newcastle, in Paris; publication of Suckling's *Fragmenta Aurea*; 1646/7 Lovelace returns to England; Thomas Browne's *Pseudodoxia Epidemica* published

1647   Scots hand Charles I over to Parliament; Charles I seized by the army; *Heads of the Proposals* presented by the army to the King; first Leveller *Agreement of the People*; Putney Debates; Leveller mutiny; Charles I escapes custody and flees to the Isle of Wight; Charles I signs Engagement with the Scots; John Wilmot (later second Earl of Rochester) born; Robert Herrick, poet, expelled from his vicarage at Dean's Prior for royalist sympathies

1648   Vote of 'No Addresses', prohibiting further negotiations with Charles I, passed by Parliament; Second Civil War; Battle of Preston, Scots defeated; Treaty of Newport negotiations; second Leveller *Agreement of the People*; Pride's Purge, Rump assumes power; Peace of Westphalia ends Thirty Years War; Herrick's *Hesperides*; Lovelace imprisoned in October, released in April 1649

1649   Trial and execution of Charles I; Charles II proclaimed in Scotland and Ireland; Rump abolishes monarchy and the House of Lords; Gerard Winstanley and the Diggers begin to cultivate lands in Surrey; England declared a Free Commonwealth; third Leveller *Agreement of the People*; Leveller mutiny; Cromwell arrives in Ireland; Richard Lovelace's *Lucasta*; death of Richard Crashaw; confiscation of Cavendish estates

1650   Rump passes Blasphemy Act; Cromwell returns from Ireland and succeeds Fairfax as commander-in-chief; Charles II lands in Scotland after swearing to the Covenant; Cromwell invades Scotland; height of the Ranter movement; height and collapse of the Diggers; Anne Bradstreet's *The Tenth Muse, Lately Sprung up in America*; publication of Vaughan's *Silex Scintellans*; 1650–2 Marvell at Fairfax' Yorkshire estate as tutor to Mary Fairfax; Marvell's 'Horatian Ode' and 'Tom May's Death'

1651 Charles II crowned King of Scots at Scone; Battle of Worcester, Charles II escapes to France; Milton's first *Defence*; Hobbes' *Leviathan*; Margaret Cavendish in England petitioning for income from husband's estates (refused); death of Lady Mary Wroth, circa 1651–3

1652 Start of war with the Dutch (to 1654); An 'Act for the Settling of Ireland' begins the Cromwellian settlement of Ireland; Quaker movement becomes well-established

1653 Cromwell expels the Rump; Barebone's Parliament, includes members from Scotland and Ireland; Instrument of Government, with Cromwell as Lord Protector; height of Fifth Monarchist movement; Walton's *Compleat Angler*; publication of Cavendish's *Poems and Fancies*; death of the royalist political theorist Sir Robert Filmer

1654 Union of Scotland and England proclaimed; first Protectorate Parliament; expedition against Spanish colonies in West Indies and mainland America

1655 Cromwell dissolves first Protectorate Parliament; royalist rebellion in Wiltshire; introduction of major-generals, given wide control over local government as well as military affairs; treaty with France, prompting exile of Stuarts from France; readmission of the Jews into England

1656 Second Protectorate Parliament; Quaker James Nayler's entry into Bristol in imitation of Christ's into Jerusalem; Cowley, *Poems, Davideis, Pindaric Odes*; Quakers arrive in Massachusetts; publication of John Harrington's *Oceana* (a republican utopia)

1657 *Humble Petition and Advice*, Cromwell refuses the Crown; major-generals abolished; death of William Harvey; death of John Lilburne; circa 1657–8 death of Lovelace; Marvell appointed Latin Secretary to the Council of State; Wren elected Professor of Anatomy at Gresham College, Oxford

1658 Second session of second Protectorate Parliament; death of Oliver Cromwell, accession of Richard

Cromwell as Lord Protector; Browne's *The Garden of Cyrus*

1659 Richard Cromwell's first parliament meets; Richard Cromwell resigns; Army recalls the Rump; royalist rebellion in Cheshire; formation of the Rota Club; publication of Suckling's *The Last Remains of Sir John Suckling*; publication of Lovelace's *Lucasta: Posthume Poems*; Marvell elected MP for Hull (remains as such for nearly 20 years); Dryden's 'Stanzas on the Death of Cromwell'

1660 General Monck's march from Scotland arrives in London; Monck readmits members of the Long Parliament excluded by Pride's Purge; the Long Parliament dissolves itself; Declaration of Breda by Charles II; Convention Parliament meets; Charles II proclaimed; Dryden's *Astraea Redux*; circa 1660 Daniel Defoe born; Pepys begins his diary; Act of Oblivion; publication of Robert Boyle's *New Experiments Physico-Mechanical*; Anne Killigrew born; Milton's *The Ready and Easy Way to Establish a Free Commonwealth*

1661 Anne Finch, Countess of Winchilsea, poet, born; James, Duke of York, marries Anne Hyde; Cavalier Parliament; Venner's Rising (Fifth Monarchist); Wren elected Professor of Astronomy at Oxford; Robert Boyle's *The Sceptical Chemist*; Anthony Ashley Cooper created Lord Ashley and Chancellor of the Exchequer; Quaker 'Peace Testimony'

1662 The Royal Society founded as reorganization of the Philosophical Society; Charles II marries Catherine of Braganza; Act of Uniformity; publication of Cavendish's *Playes* and *Orations of Divers Sorts*; Boyle's Law; Act of Settlement in Ireland

1663 Butler's *Hudibras* (part I); Drury Lane Theatre built (first called the Theatre Royal); first attempt to impeach Clarendon

1664 Thomas Browne elected Fellow of the Royal College of Physicians and testifies at a witch trial at Bury St Edmunds; publication of Cavendish's *Philosophical*

Letters and *CCXI Sociable Letters*; unauthorized edition of Katherine Philips' *Poems*; death of Philips

1665 Great Plague of London; second Dutch War (to 1667)

1666 Great Fire of London; publication of Cavendish's *The Description of a New World, called the Blazing World*

1667 Jonathan Swift born; Sprat's *History of the Royal Society*; first edition of Milton's *Paradise Lost* in 10 books; death of Abraham Cowley; Dutch attack in the Medway; Dryden's *Annus Mirabilis* and *Essay on Dramatic Poesy*; posthumous edition of Philips' poems and translations; Clarendon impeached, flees to France

1668 Dryden appointed Poet Laureate; James secretly converts to Catholicism

1669 Death of William Prynne; Wren becomes Surveyor of the Royal Works; Dryden's *Tyrannic Love* (heroic drama)

1670 William Congreve born; Lord Ashley supports call to legitimize Monmouth; first performance of a play by Behn, *The Forced Marriage*; Dryden's *The Conquest of Granada* (heroic drama)

1671 Milton's *Paradise Regained* and *Samson Agonistes*; Thomas Browne knighted during a visit by Charles II to Norwich

1672 Joseph Addison and Richard Steele born; Marvell's *The Rehearsal Transposed* (first part); Declaration of Indulgence; third Dutch War, to 1674; Lord Ashley made Lord Chancellor and created 1st Earl of Shaftesbury; death of the painter Samuel Cooper

1673 Marvell's *The Rehearsal Transposed* (second part); withdrawal of Declaration of Indulgence; Test Act; death of Cavendish; Wren knighted

1674 Wycherley's *The Plain-Dealer* (comedy); second, 12-book edition of Milton's *Paradise Lost*; deaths of Milton and Herrick

1675 Wycherley's *The Country Wife* (comedy); Dryden's *Aureng-Zebe* (heroic drama); Wren's rebuilding of St Paul's begins; circa 1675, death of Lucy Hutchinson

1676 Etheredge's *The Man of Mode, or Sir Fopling Flutter* (comedy)

1677 Marvell's *An Account of the Growth of Popery and Arbitrary Government* (published anonymously); Mary married to William of Orange; Shaftesbury and other Whigs imprisoned; Behn's *The Rover*

1678 Bunyan's *Pilgrim's Progress* (part I); Dryden's *All for Love*; Popish Plot; Marvell dies; Vaughan's *Thalia Rediviva*; second Test Act excludes Catholics from Parliament and the court

1679 Death of Hobbes; Parliament dissolved as it discusses the succession

1680 Rochester dies; Exclusion Bill; Parliament again dissolved for discussing the succession; Charles enters into informal, secret agreement with Louis XIV (Treaty of Dover); posthumous publication of Sir Robert Filmer's *Patriarcha*; death of the painter Sir Peter Lely (knighted in same year)

1681 Dryden's *Absalom and Achitophel*; posthumous publication of Marvell's *Miscellaneous Poems*; Shaftesbury charged with treason, is released by a Whig grand jury in London

1682 Thomas Otway's *Venice Preserved* (tragedy); Dryden's 'MacFlecknoe'; death of Sir Thomas Browne; Shaftesbury flees to Holland

1683 A purported Protestant conspiracy (the Rye House Plot) to assassinate Charles II and James discovered; Shaftesbury dies in Holland

1684 Publication of Behn's *Poems Upon Several Occasions* and part one of *Love Letters Between a Nobleman and his Sister*

1685 John Gay born; Charles II dies and James II accedes to the throne with no overt opposition; Monmouth's Rebellion; William sends troops to aid in suppressing Monmouth's Rebellion; James opens diplomatic correspondence and exchanges envoys with the Vatican; Dryden converts to Catholicism; death of the poet Anne Killigrew

1686 *Godden v. Hales* confirms the king's right to dispense with the Test Act; establishment of Commission for Ecclesiastical Causes; 1686–8 Archbishopric of

York vacant as James seeks appointment of Catholic bishops; Edmund Waller's *Poems*; posthumous publication of *Poems by Mrs. Anne Killigrew*

1687 Newton's *Principia* (Latin); Dryden's *The Hind and the Panther*; James' Declaration of Indulgence; Parliament dissolved; Mary of Modena's pregnancy announced in December

1688 Death of Bunyan; Alexander Pope born; Behn's *Oroonoko* and *The Fair Jilt*; birth of James Francis Edward, Prince of Wales; William 'invited' on 30 June and James II flees to France

1689 William and Mary take the throne; Lady Mary Wortley Montagu born; Samuel Richardson born; death of Behn; Bill of Rights, political foundation of the Glorious Revolution

GLOSSARY OF KEY TERMS AND CONCEPTS

Allegory
A type of narrative, in verse or prose, in which the surface story – of interest in and of itself – conveys a higher meaning in terms of ideas. In other words, the surface narrative is an extended analogy that personifies abstract ideas outside the text. Hence, there is political, social and religious allegory, all of which are evident in Milton's *Paradise Lost*. Bunyan's *Pilgrim's Progress*, on the surface, is the story of Christian, whose spiritual journey towards salvation is an allegory for that of all Christians.

Aphorism
A concise statement or sentence providing a principle of conduct or moral direction. Bacon's prose style in his *Essays* is aphorisitic.

Baroque
An artistic movement, primarily continental, which may be characterized as an attempt to capture the physical tensions

of dynamic movement and mass in painting and sculpture. It is also naturalistic in its approach, as opposed to the tranquillity and mathematical perspective of its Renaissance artistic precursors. The most notable Baroque artists are the painter Caravaggio (1571–1610) and the sculptor Giovanni Bernini (1598–1680). Crashaw is the English writer most indebted to the Baroque, but its influence is evident even in Milton's *Paradise Lost*.

Comedy

Broadly defined (as there are many forms: i.e. city comedy, comedy of manners), the dramatic genre is one of humour and entertainment – but not without a didactic intent, particularly through satire. Generally, as opposed to tragedy comedy deals with lower-class characters and everyday life, often in a domestic setting. It explores human vices and frailties, and, importantly, has a happy ending (conventionally through the marriage of its central couple, which acts as a symbolic form of social reconciliation).

Country-house poem

A poem which praises the estate and family of a man of high social standing. Linked to the pastoral, the genre praises a way of life, viewing the estate and its owner as a microcosmic representation of a well-ordered society. It also allowed poets to negotiate patronage relationships. See, for example, Lanyer's 'The Description of Cooke-ham', Jonson's 'To Penshurst' and Marvell's 'Upon Appleton House'.

Elegy

A poem written to mourn the death of an individual (either a personal acquaintance or an important personage). It is formal and elevated in style, generally expressing grief at the loss of the individual, praise of his or her accomplishments, a meditation on death and, often, a reaffirmation of immortality that provides a transcendent significance to the individual's death. See, for example, Marvell's 'An Elegy upon the Death of My Lord Francis Villiers' and Milton's pastoral elegy, 'Lycidas'. Like 'sonnet', elegy was a term applied not only to the definition just provided, but also for love complaints, such as Donne's elegies.

Epic

A long narrative poem, usually divided into books or cantos, written in an elevated style. It focuses on the heroic accomplishments of figures of national significance or, in the case of Milton's *Paradise Lost* and *Paradise Regained*, the human race. Vast settings, superhuman courage and supernatural intervention are common elements. The classical models provided by the Greek poet Homer and the Roman poet Virgil are evident not only in the genre's focus on heroism, but also in the epic poet's invocation of a Muse and beginning the narrative *in medias res* ('in the middle of things').

Epigram

A concise, often antithetical poem. Originally, epigram meant a short inscription on a monument. This sense of memorializing is evident in epigrams of the period: notably, those of Donne and Jonson. The epigram was also an effective form for satirical purposes.

Heroic drama

A dramatic genre which came to dominate the Restoration stage. It is marked by bombastic dialogue, exotic and spectacular settings, the hero's conflicting views of love and honour, a heroine too virtuous to be real and a banally evil villain.

History play

A type of drama dealing with a historical or legendary personage (usually a king) of national significance. While it was a significant genre in the closing decades of the sixteenth century, there are few examples in the seventeenth century. See, for example, Ford's *Perkin Warbeck*.

Mock-heroic

A parody, often in miniature, of the epic and its conventions. It is an effective means of satirizing a subject or individual by elevating the ridiculous to epic proportions. Rochester's 'Disabled Debauchee' is a short example, while Samuel Butler's *Hudibras* (Part I, 1661) attains to the length of an epic.

Muses

Nine goddesses who preside over poetry, music, history, drama, dance and astronomy. They are usually described as the daughters of Zeus and Mnemosyne (Memory). Conventionally, poets appealed to a Muse for inspiration and aid in writing. Milton, for example, invokes Calliope (Muse of epic poetry) and Urania (Muse of astronomy) in *Paradise Lost*.

Ode

A form of lyric, most often occasional. It treats its subject in a dignified language and tone. There are three types, each identified by its complex stanzaic forms: Pindaric (two stanza types), Horatian (one stanza type) and Irregular. Examples include Jonson's 'Ode on Cary and Morison', Behn's odes on the death of the Earl of Rochester and Charles II, Marvell's ode on Cromwell and numerous poems by Cowley.

Panegyric

A formal, occasional poem or prose work that praises an individual. It is related to *encomium*, a composition praising a living person or an event.

Pastoral

Very strictly defined, a poem dealing with shepherds and the rustic life in the tradition of the Roman poet Virgil's *Eclogues*. Classical pastoral encompassed love complaints, panegyric and elegy as well as singing matches pitting together two poet-shepherds. More broadly speaking, however, the pastoral deals with an artificial, idealized life – positing a critical contrast between city and countryside, the latter often a world experiencing a perpetual, fecund spring and peace. It was a prevalent type of poetry in the seventeenth century and its conventions are present in any number of genres: the country-house poem, occasional verse, drama and prose romance. Often, Christian writers, particularly Puritans, utilized the biblical analogies of Christ as shepherd (Latin, *pastor*) to include satirical anti-clerical elements, as well as to assert the triumph of Christianity over 'paganism' by contrasting the superiority of Eden over the classical Golden Age. Cavaliers were more prone to retain, through Jonson's classicism, a sense of the Golden Age.

Petrarchan conventions
The work of the fourteenth-century Italian poet Petrarch was introduced into England in the early sixteenth century. The conceits of his sonnets were widely imitated throughout the Elizabethan period and were often mocked by Jacobean writers such as Donne and Lady Mary Wroth. The Petrarchan conceit consists of hyperbolic analogies to describe a male lover's emotional turmoil and despair prompted by the 'cruelty' of his female beloved.

Platonism
Based on the idealist philosophy of Plato, Platonism in seventeenth-century literature is most apparent in regards to love. Essentially positing a distinction between a lower and higher form of love, the soul of a Platonic lover embarks on a quest to reach his spiritual home by transcending the sensual love of individual, female beauty (which decays) and attaining to a virtuous love of immutable, divine beauty. Platonism is evident in Carew's verse and Caroline masques.

Romance
A literary work with extravagant characters, exotic locales and heroic events. A romance plot is generally driven by passionate love. Examples can be found in poetry, drama and prose in the seventeenth century: in poetry, the

representation of Satan in Milton's *Paradise Lost* owes much to romance; in drama, Shakespeare's late plays, including *The Tempest*; and in prose romance, the most prevalent form, particularly during the Restoration, numerous works by Behn.

Satire

Essentially a didactic genre, the satirist's aim is to improve his or her society by critically focusing on human frailties and vices with the intention to prompt social change. Satire can be direct (when a first-person speaker addresses the reader or a character in the satire), for example, Marvell's 'Last Instructions to a Painter'; or indirect, where the narrative or actions and dialogue of characters conveys the author's satirical intent, as in Robert Burton's *Anatomy of Melancholy* (1626). In addition, critics further distinguish satirists by their tone – Juvenalian and Horatian, named after the two great classical satirists, Juvenal and Horace. Juvenalian satire is harsh and invective, verging, at times, on misanthropy; Horatian is much gentler and more reliant on a restrained humour. Rochester's satire is Juvenalian, while Dryden's is Horatian.

Sonnet

A lyric poem consisting of 14 lines of iambic pentameter. There are two basic types, named after their most famous practitioners: the Petrarchan and the Shakespearean. The Petrarchan sonnet is divided into an octave (eight lines) and a sestet (six lines). Each division has its own rhyme scheme, but a proper Petrarchan sonnet will not end with a couplet. The Shakespearean sonnet consists of three quatrains (each with two rhymes) and ends with a couplet. Milton and Lady Mary Wroth, for example, wrote sonnets in the Petrarchan form. It is important to note that, in the seventeenth century, any short lyric was often called a sonnet; hence, Donne's *Songs and Sonnets* (1633) and Suckling's 'sonnets'.

Tragedy

In drama especially, tragedy deals with characters of high social standing. Following, broadly, from Aristotle's definition of the term in his *Poetics*, the tragic hero moves from happiness to misery through some flaw in his or her character. The plot is driven by the consequences of the protagonist's flaw and, after experiencing an epiphany (itself a tragic recognition of responsibility), the hero's death.

Typology

A form of biblical exegesis in which persons and events in the Old Testament foreshadow those of the New Testament. For example, Samson in the Old Testament is a 'type' of Christ. Dryden's *Absalom and Achitophel* extensively uses typology to associate King David with Charles II.

FURTHER READING AND RESOURCES

Further reading

Reference

Hornblower, S. and Spawforth, A. (eds) (1999) *The Oxford Classical Dictionary* (3rd edn). Oxford: Oxford University Press. Invaluable for researching classical allusions.

Oxford English Dictionary (1989) (2nd edn), 20 vols. Oxford: Oxford University Press.

History

Akrigg, G. P. V. (1974) *Jacobean Pageant: The court of King James I*. New York: Atheneum. Akrigg covers the politics and religion of the period and provides a sense of the day-to-day affairs of the Jacobean court through its many colourful personalities. The book is a bit dated, however, and should be supplemented with Cruickshanks' collection below.

Corns, T. N. (ed.) (1999) *The Royal Image: Representations of Charles I*. Cambridge: Cambridge University Press. The essays collected here, both by literary critics and historians, cover all aspects of court and popular representations of Charles I – from masques to coinage.

Cruickshanks, E. (ed.) (2000) *The Stuart Courts*. Thrupp: Sutton

Publishing. Individual essays provide well-researched arguments, from a variety of historical perspectives, on the political, religious and cultural events of the reigns of all the Stuart monarchs discussed in this book.

Hill, C. (1972) *The World Turned Upside Down: Radical ideas during the English Revolution*. London: Maurice Temple Smith. Hill has written many books on the seventeenth century, and his leftist perspective results here in a fascinating analysis of radical political and religious groups of the 1640s and 1650s.

Kelsey, S. (1997) *Inventing a Republic: The political culture of the English Commonwealth, 1649–1653*. Manchester: Manchester University Press. Perhaps one of the best analyses of the attempt to fashion the Commonwealth into a republic. Kelsey devotes chapters to Parliament's careful handling of iconography, spectacle, politics and honour.

Kishlansky, M. (1996) *A Monarchy Transformed: Britain 1603–1714*. Harmondsworth: Penguin. This is an accessible, straightforward historical narrative of the Stuart monarchies in the Penguin History of Britain series. It is a good place to start for an historical overview of the period.

McGregor, J. F. and Reay, B. (eds) (1984) *Radical Religion in the English Revolution*. Oxford: Oxford University Press. The essays collected by McGregor and Reay cover all the significant religious sects of the seventeenth century – both in terms of how the individual sects defined themselves and how others saw them.

Miller, J. (1973) *Popery and Politics in England, 1660–1688*. Cambridge: Cambridge University Press. A very detailed examination of anti-Catholicism in English politics during the reigns of Charles II and James II.

Morril, J. (2002) *Stuart Britain: A very short introduction*. Oxford: Oxford University Press. Morril's brief introduction to the period, like Kishlansky's lengthier treatment above, is a starting point before embarking on more in-depth research on particular people, movements and events.

Pocock, J. G. A. (2003) (rpt) *The Machiavellian Moment: Florentine political thought and the Atlantic Republican Tradition*. Princeton: Princeton University Press. This is the most comprehensive appraisal of republican thought. Beginning with the foundational Italian republics, Pocock moves on to consider the influence of those political ideals in England and beyond.

Sharpe, K. (1989) *Politics and Ideas in Early Stuart England: Essays and studies*. London and New York: Pinter Publishers. One of the most important historians of the period, Sharpe brings a remarkable critical acumen to both issues and personalities of the Jacobean and Caroline periods.

Stone, L. (1965) *The Crisis of the Aristocracy, 1558–1641*. Oxford: Clarendon Press. Stone's magisterial work on the political and economic problems facing the aristocracy is supported by numerous charts and statistical breakdowns. Fortunately, especially for students of literature, it is available in an abridged edition, cited here.

Tuck, R. (2002) *Hobbes: A very short introduction*. Oxford: Oxford University Press. This brief introduction to one of the key thinkers of the period provides both biographical information as well as the intellectual context of Hobbes' radical ideas.

Wedgewood, C. V. (1955) *The Kings Peace, 1637–1641*. London: Collins Fontana; (1958) *The King's War, 1641–1647*. London: Collins; (1964) *The Trial of Charles I*. London: Macmillan. Wedgewood's trilogy provides a wonderfully readable narrative account of the reign of Charles I from just prior to the Bishops' Wars to his execution.

Woolrych, A. (1982) *Commonwealth to Protectorate*. Oxford: Clarendon Press. A very well-researched and detailed account of Parliament's struggle to find a political settlement.

Literary criticism

The following bibliography is limited, almost primarily, to selected works not cited in this book.

Achinstein, S. (1994) *Milton and the Revolutionary Reader*. Princeton: Princeton University Press. Achinstein's scope here is much wider than Milton, as she explores how writers took advantage of the lapse in censorship to construct a politicized readership – a revolutionary public sphere.

Brooks, D. A. (2000) *From Playhouse to Printing House: Drama and authorship in early modern England*. Cambridge: Cambridge University Press. The first of Brooks' examination of early modern print culture. Though focusing on the publication of plays, his insights go beyond that particular genre.

Chernaik, W. (1995) *Sexual Freedom in Restoration Literature*. Cambridge: Cambridge University Press. Chapters in this book deal with contexts and less familiar works, as well as Rochester, Dryden and Behn. The readings are especially attuned to the politics of libertinism.

Goldberg, J. (1983) *James I and the Politics of Literature: Jonson, Shakespeare, Donne and their contemporaries*. Baltimore: Johns Hopkins University Press. An early example of New Historicist criticism, Goldberg wonderfully reads the politics of representation in literature and kingship.

Knoppers, L. L. (1994) *Historicizing Milton: Spectacle, Power, and Poetry in Restoration England*. Athens, GA and London: University of Georgia Press. Knoppers reads Milton and his contemporaries, both supporters of the 'Good Old Cause' and royalists, against Restoration politics and displays of authority.

Norbrook, D. (1999) *Writing the English Republic: Poetry, rhetoric, and politics, 1627–1660*. Cambridge: Cambridge University Press. Like Kelsey's treatment of Parliament's attempt to 'invent' a republic, Norbrook explores both republican theorists and writers who attempted to create the cultural forms that could sustain 'liberty'.

Pacheco, A. (ed.) (1992) *Early Women Writers: 1600–1720*. London and New York: Longman. This collection contains essays on both contexts and individual authors.

Raymond, J. (ed) (1993) *Making the News: An anthology of the newsbooks of revolutionary England 1641–1660*. Moreton-in-Marsh: Windrush Press. If one is unable to gain access to either microfilm collections or web-based primary documents, Raymond's anthology of newsbook selections is a useful resource. Accounts of the most significant events provide a sense of the polemical context of such publications.

Summers, C. J. and Pebworth, T. (eds) (1993) *Renaissance Discourses of Desire*. Columbia and London: University of Missouri Press.

The representation of desire in literature, across genres, is quite comprehensively covered by the essays collected in this volume, both in terms of literary tradition and politics.

Turner, J. G. (2002) *Libertines and Radicals in Early Modern London: Sexuality, politics and literary culture, 1630–1685*. Cambridge: Cambridge University Press. This is a much more radical consideration – not only in terms of its conclusions, but also theoretically – of libertinism than Chernaik's book cited above. Turner explores the literature and politics of the period through the interaction of popular culture and the aristocracy.

Veevers, E. (1989) *Images of Love and Religion: Queen Henrietta Maria and court entertainments*. Cambridge: Cambridge University Press. Veevers provides an account of the continental influences of Caroline court culture introduced by the queen. Chapters deal not only with French traditions, but also with their adaptation by English writers as well as the reaction of Puritan polemicists.

Zwicker, S. (1993) *Lines of Authority: Politics and English literary culture, 1649–1689*. Ithaca: Cornell University Press. The links between politics and literature are treated here in terms of similarities in representation. The chapter on the Restoration is particularly insightful.

There are a number of relevant volumes in the Cambridge Companion series. In each, the contributors address wider contexts – such as gender and religion – as well as individual authors and their work. The most notable for our period are:

Corns, T. N. (ed.) (1997) *The Cambridge Companion to English Poetry, Donne to Marvell*. Cambridge: Cambridge University Press.

Fisk, D. (ed.) (2000) *The Cambridge Companion to English Restoration Theatre*. Cambridge: Cambridge University Press.

Keeble, N. H. (ed.) (2001) *The Cambridge Companion to Writing of the English Revolution*. Cambridge: Cambridge University Press.

Web-based resources

Early Modern Literary Studies (www.shu.ac.uk/emls/emlshome.html) includes links to the journal's archive, as well as to sites relating to the history and literature of the sixteenth and seventeenth centuries. In addition, there is a link to *Early Stuart Libels*, Alastair Bellany and Andrew McRae (eds) (www.earlystuartlibels.net/htdocs/index.htm), covering publications from 1603–42.

Literature Compass (www.literature-compass.com) provides excellent reviews of recent publications along with other information useful to students of seventeenth-century literature.

The Luminarium site (www.luminarium.org/sevenlit/) contains not only the works of individual authors, but also critical essays. In addition, there are links to other seventeenth-century resources relating to the history, culture and literature of the period.

The following web-resources can only be accessed if your college or university subscribes to them.

Oxford English Dictionary Online. A wonderful resource for understanding the contemporary nuance of words. Each entry provides examples of historical usage. If it is not available online, then most libraries have the published form: (1989) *Oxford English Dictionary* (2nd edn), 20 vols. Oxford: Oxford University Press.

Early English Books Online. An amazing resource for a wide variety of primary documents, including royal proclamations, parliamentary orders, newsbooks and a wide range of authors on diverse topics, including, of course, literature. It contains works from the 'Pollard & Redgrave Short-title Catalogue', 'Wing's Short-title Catalogue' and the 'Thomason Tracts'.

References

Achinstein, S. (1994) *Milton and the Revolutionary Reader*. Princeton: Princeton University Press.

Adamson, J. (2000) 'The kingdoms of England and Great Britain: The Tudor and Stuart courts, 1509–1714', in Adamson, J. (ed.), *The Princely Courts of Europe, 1500–1750*. London: Cassell & Co., pp. 95–117.

Ashton, R. (ed.) (1969) *James I by his Contemporaries*. London: Hutchinson & Co.

Aubrey, J. (1957) 'Mr. John Milton', in Hughes, M. Y. (ed.), *John Milton: Complete Poems and Major Prose*. New York: Macmillan, pp. 1021–25.

Bacon, F. (1939a) *Novum Organum*, in Burtt, E. A. (ed.), *The English Philosophers from Bacon to Mill*. New York: Random House, pp. 24–123.

Bacon, F. (1939b) *The Great Instauration*, in Burtt, E. A. (ed.), *The English Philosophers from Bacon to Mill*. New York: Random House, pp. 5–23.

Bacon, F. (1995) *Essays*. New York: Prometheus Books.

Bacon, F. (2000) *New Atlantis*, in Bowerbank, S. and Mendelson, S. (eds), *Paper Bodies: A Margaret Cavendish reader*. Peterborough: Broadview Press, pp. 264–300.

Beaumont, F. (1970) edited by Bradbrook, M. C., *Beaumont and Fletcher: Selected plays*. London: Everyman.

Beecher, D. (1992) 'Introduction', in Beecher, D. (ed.), *Barnabe Riche, His Farewell to Military Profession*. Ottawa: Dovehouse Editions, pp. 13–120.

Behn, A. (1998) in Salzman, P. (ed.), *Oroonoko and Other Writings*. Oxford: Oxford University Press.

Boswell, J. (1980) *Christianity, Social Tolerance, and Homosexuality: Gay people in Western Europe from the beginning of the christian era to the fourteenth century*. Chicago: University of Chicago Press.

Bradley, A. C. (1971) *Shakespearean Tragedy* (2nd edn). London: St Martin's Press.

Bray, A. (1995) *Homosexuality in Renaissance England* (2nd edn). New York: Columbia University Press.

Breitenberg, M. (1996) *Anxious Masculinity in Early Modern England*. Cambridge: Cambridge University Press.

Cavendish, M. (2000) edited by Bowerbank, S. and Mendelson, S., *Paper Bodies: A Margaret Cavendish reader*. Peterborough: Broadview Press.

Charles I (attr John Gauden) (2005) edited by Daems, J. and Nelson, H., *Eikon Basilike with Selections from Eikonoklastes*. Peterborough: Broadview Press.

Clark, S. (1995) ' "Something generous in mere lust?": Rochester and misogyny', in Burns, E. (ed.) *Reading Rochester*. Liverpool: Liverpool University Press, pp. 21–41.

Cleveland, J. (1647) *The Character of a London Diurnall*. London.

Corns, T. N. (1992) *Uncloistered Virtue: English Political Literature, 1640–1660*. Oxford: Clarendon Press.

Craftie Cromwell: or, Oliver ordering our New State. A Tragi-Comedie (1648). London.

Crashaw, R. (1974) edited by Williams, G. W., The Complete Poetry of Richard Crashaw. New York: W. W. Norton & Co.

Daems, J. and Nelson, H. (2005) 'Introduction', in Daems, J. and Nelson, H. (eds), *Eikon Basilike with Selections from Eikonoklastes*. Peterborough: Broadview Press, pp. 13–39.

Dollimore, J. and Sinfield, A. (1994) 'Introduction: Shakespeare, cultural materialism and the new historicism', in Dollimore, J. and Sinfield, A. (eds), *Political Shakespeare: Essays in Cultural Materialism* (2nd edn). Ithaca: Cornell University Press, pp. 2–17.

Dryden, J. (1985) edited by Miner, E., *Selected Poetry and Prose of John Dryden*. New York: Random House.

Eliot, T. S. (1963) (rpt) edited by Hayward, J., *Selected Prose*. Harmondsworth: Penguin.

Evans, J. M. (1996) *Milton's Imperial Epic: Paradise Lost and the discourse of colonialism*. Ithaca: Cornell University Press.

Faderman, L. (1981) *Surpassing the Love of Men: Romantic friendship and love between women from the Renaissance to the present*. New York: Morrow.

Gallagher, C. (1988) 'Embracing the absolute: Margaret Cavendish and the politics of the female subject in seventeenth-century England', *Genders*, I, (1), 24–33.

Gardiner, S. G. (ed.) (1951) *The Constitutional Documents of the Puritan Revolution, 1625–1660* (3rd edn, rpt). Oxford: Clarendon Press.

Goldberg, J. (1992) *Sodometrics: Renaissance texts, modern sexualities*. Stanford: Stanford University Press.

Greenblatt, S., Cohen, W. Howard, J. E. and Eisaman Maus, K. (eds) (1997) *The Norton Shakespeare*. New York: W. W. Norton.

Halley, J. E. (1994) '*Bowers v. Hardwick* in the renaissance', in Goldberg, J. (ed.), *Queering the Renaissance*. Durham and London: Duke University Press, pp. 15–33.

Hammond, P. (1991) 'The king's two bodies: representations of Charles II', in Black, J. and Gregory, J. (eds), *Culture, Politics and Society in Britain, 1660–1800*. Manchester: Manchester University Press, pp. 13–48.

Harris, B. (ed.) (1953) *Restoration Plays*. New York: Random House.

Harrison, G. B. (1956) *Elizabethan Plays & Players*. Ann Arbor: University of Michigan Press.

Hill, C. (2001) (rpt) *Puritanism & Revolution: Studies in interpretation of the English Revolution of the 17th Century*. London: Pimlico.

Hobbes, T. (1988) (rpt) edited by Macpherson, C. B., *Leviathan*. Harmondsworth: Penguin.

Hoby, E. (1997) 'The politics of gender', in Corns, T. N. (ed.), *The Cambridge Companion to English Poetry: Donne to Marvell*. Cambridge: Cambridge University Press, pp. 31–51.

Howarth, D. (1993) 'The politics of Inigo Jones', in Howarth, D. (ed.), *Art and Patronage in the Caroline Courts: Essays in honour of Sir Oliver Millar*. Cambridge: Cambridge University Press. pp. 68–89.

Hutchinson, L. (1995) edited by Keeble, N. H., *Memoirs of the Life of Colonel Hutchinson*. London: J. M. Dent.

Hutton, R. (1987) *The Restoration: A political and religious history of England and Wales, 1658–1667*. Oxford: Oxford University Press.

James I. (1996) edited by Fischlin, D. and Fortier, M., *The True Law of Free Monarchies and Basilikon Doron*. Toronto: Centre for Reformation and Renaissance Studies.

Johnson, S. (1958) edited by Bronson, B. H., *Samuel Johnson: Rasselas, poems, and selected prose*. New York: Holt, Rinehart and Winston.

Jonson, B. (1996) (rpt) edited by Parfitt, G., *Ben Jonson: the Complete Poems*. Harmondsworth: Penguin.

Kahn, V. (1997) 'Margaret Cavendish and the romance of contract', *Renaissance Quarterly*, 50, 526–66.

Kelsey, S. (1997) *Inventing a Republic: The political culture of the English Commonwealth, 1649–1653*. Stanford: Stanford University Press.

Kenyon, J. P. (1982) *The Stuarts: A Study in English Kingship*. Glasgow: William Collins Sons & Co.

Kishlansky, M. (1996) *A Monarchy Transformed: Britain 1603–1714*. Harmondsworth: Penguin.

Knights, L. C. (1971) (rpt) '*King Lear* and the great tragedies', in Ford, B. (ed.), *The Pelican Guide to English Literature*. Harmondsworth: Penguin, pp. 228–56.

Lady Falkland: Her Life (1994) in Weller, B. and Ferguson, M. W. (eds), *The Tradegy of Mariam, the Fair Queen of Jewry (with The Lady Falkland): Her Life, by One of Her Daughters*. Berkeley: University of California Press, pp. 183–275.

Levine, L. (1994) *Men in Women's Clothing: Anti-theatricality and Effeminization, 1579–1642*. Cambridge: Cambridge University Press.

Lindley, D. (ed.) (1998) *Court Masques*. Oxford: Oxford University Press.

Locke, J. (1952) edited by Peardon, T. P., *The Second Treatise of Government*. Indianapolis: Bobbs-Merrill.

Loewenstein, D. (1990) *Milton and the Drama of History: Historical vision, iconoclasm, and the literary imagination*. Cambridge: Cambridge University Press.

Maclean, H. (ed.) (1974) *Ben Jonson and the Cavalier Poets*. New York: W. W. Norton.

Madan, F. F. (1950) *A New Bibliography of the Eikon Basilike of King Charles the First; with a Note on the Authorship*. London: B. Quaritch.

Madway, L. (2000) ' "The most conspicuous solemnity": the coronation of Charles II', in Cruickshanks, E. (ed.), *The Stuart Courts*. Thrupp: Sutton Publishing, pp. 141–57.

Martz, L. L. (1962) *The Poetry of Meditation: A study in English religious literature of the seventeenth century* (rev. edn). New Haven and London: Yale University Press.

Milton, J. (1953–1982) *The First Defence*, in Wolfe, D. M. (ed.), *The Complete Prose Works of John Milton* (8 vols), vol. 4. New Haven: Yale University Press.

Milton, J. (1991) in Orgel, S. and Goldberg, J. (eds), *John Milton: A Critical Edition of the Major Works*. Oxford: Oxford University Press.

Milton, J. (2005) *Eikonoklastes*, in Daems, J. and Nelson, H. (eds), *Eikon Basilike with Selections from Eikonoklastes*. Peterborough: Broadview Press.

Miner, E. (1974) 'The Cavalier ideal of the good life', in Maclean, H. (ed.), *Ben Jonson and the Cavalier Poets*. New York: W. W. Norton, pp. 465–79.

Moretti, F. (2005) Signs Taken for Wonders: On the sociology of literary forms. London: Verso.

Patrides, C. A. (1977) 'Above Atlas his shoulders: An introduction to Sir Thomas Browne', in Patrides, C. A. (ed.), *Sir Thomas Browne: The major works*. Harmondsworth: Penguin, pp. 21–52.

Pepys, S. (1960) edited by Morshead, O. F., *The Diary of Samuel Pepys*. New York: Harper & Row.

Phillips, E. (1957) 'The life of Milton', in Hughes, M. Y. (ed.), *John Milton: Complete poems and major prose*. New York: Macmillan, pp. 1025–37.

Pocock, J. G. A. (2003) *The Machiavellian Moment: Florentine political thought and the Atlantic republican tradition* (2nd edn). Princeton: Princeton University Press.

Potter, L. (1989) *Secret Rites and Secret Writing: Royalist literature, 1641–1660*. Cambridge: Cambridge University Press.

Raymond, J. (1996) *The Invention of the Newspaper: English newsbooks 1641–1649*. Oxford: Clarendon Press.

Rochester, 2nd Earl of (1968) edited by Vieth, D. M., *The Works of the Earl of Rochester*. New Haven and London: Yale University Press.

Rudrum, A., Nelson, H. and Black, S. (eds) (2001a) *The Broadview Anthology of Seventeenth-Century Verse & Prose* (2 vols). *Volume I: Verse*. Peterborough: Broadview Press.

Rudrum, A., Nelson H. and Black, S. (eds) (2001b) *The Broadview*

Anthology of Seventeenth-Century Verse & Prose (2 vols). *Volume II: Prose*. Peterborough: Broadview Press.

Shakespeare, W. (1997), in Greenblatt, S. *et al.* (eds), *The Norton Shakespeare*. New York: W. W. Norton.

Sharpe, K. (1989) *Politics and Ideas in Early Stuart England: Essays and Studies*. New York and London: Pinter Publishers.

Sidney, P. (1983) edited by Kimbrough, R., *Sir Philip Sidney: Selected Prose and Poetry* (2nd edn). Madison: University of Wisconsin Press.

Smith, N. (1994) *Literature and Revolution in England, 1640–1660*. New Haven and London: Yale University Press.

Taylor, J. (1990) edited by Carroll, T. K., *Jeremy Taylor: Selected Works*. New York: Paulist Press.

Tillyard, E. M. W. (1972) (rpt) *The Elizabethan World Picture*. Harmondsworth: Penguin.

Traub, V. (1992) *Desire and Anxiety: Circulations of sexuality in Shakespearean drama*. New York and London: Routledge.

Tyacke, N. (1978) (rpt) 'Puritanism, Arminianism and counter-revolution', in Russell, C. (ed.), *The Origins of the English Civil War*. London: Macmillan, pp. 119–43.

Underdown, D. (1987) *Revel, Riot, and Rebellion: Popular politics and culture in England, 1603–1660*. Oxford: Oxford University Press.

Watkin, D. (2001) *English Architecture: A concise history*. London: Thames & Hudson.

Willey, B. (1953) *The Seventeenth-Century Background: The thought of the age in relation to religion and poetry*. New York: Anchor Books.

Williams, A. P. (ed.) (1999) *The Image of Manhood in Early Modern Literature: Viewing the male*. London: Greenwood Press.

Wiseman, S. J. (1998) *Drama and Politics in the English Civil War*. Cambridge: Cambridge University Press.

Index